FROM DREAMING TO DONE

A Soul Map For Finishing What You Were Born To Do

NADIA S. KRAUSS

 LUCKY BOOK PUBLISHING

To request permissions, contact the publisher at
hello@luckybookpublishing.com.

Paperback ISBN: 978-1-997775-16-4
Hardcover ISBN: 978-1-997775-15-7
E-book ISBN: 978-1-997775-14-0

First edition, October 2025

MY GIFT TO YOU

I am so glad you're here!

As a special gift,

enjoy **FREE access** to your Soul Map Gift:
A 10-minute ritual for returning to your dreams.

https://bit.ly/SoulMapGift

PRAISE FOR DREAMING TO DONE

Turning Precious Gifts into Living Dreams!

From Dreaming to Done creates a bridge for those precious gifts we carry within to find their way out into the world, so we can finally see our dreams mirrored in reality.

- Laura Hollick, Artist & Creator of the Soul Art® process

What a powerful guidebook!

What a gift this book is! So many of my clients have been caught at one stage or another with making their big ideas real. Through the power of story, personal experience, and powerful exercises Nadia Krauss has brought into being a powerful guidebook keeping inspiration alive. She knows how to help you fan your own flames, shining light where it is needed, and prompting you forward. A dream not realized keeps you in a state of longing. This book can show you the way out of that kind of stuckness. We need this.

- Laurie Seymour, Founder/CEO at The Baca Institute

Medicine for the highly sensitive soul!

Nadia Krauss has written the book I wish I'd had during my own spiral dance between dreaming and doing. This isn't another manifesting manual or productivity hack; it's a soul map for the woman who's tired of circling her deepest calling and ready to finally land it.

What strikes me most about Nadia's approach is her unflinching honesty about the messy, non-linear path of bringing dreams to life. She doesn't promise quick fixes or bypass the emotional work required for true transformation. Instead, she offers something far more valuable: a framework rooted in embodied wisdom, gentle courage, and the kind of self-love leadership that actually sustains long-term change.

From Dreaming to Done is medicine for the highly sensitive soul who's been everything for everyone else and is finally ready to be everything for herself. If you've ever felt the ache of an unlived dream, this book will meet you exactly where you are and walk you home to yourself.

- Hal S. Eisenberg, L.M.S.W., CEO Eisenberg Leadership, Inc., Bestselling Author, Whispers in the Rain: 48 Lessons on the Roadmap to Love and Enlightenment

From Dreaming to Done is true soul food!

This gem of a read reminded me to get back to a way of being and to stop measuring life against my to do list. Thank you Nadia for guiding me home to my body and its somatic messages. Nadia's guide to soul alignment reminds me to stay rooted in my progress and to remember I am on soul time. The creator and artist of my life. Nadia's Soul Map is a powerful and moving answer for those looking to finish what they started.

- Joanne Clark, Bestselling Author of Exquisitely Bored, Fractional CMO

It felt like an energetic hug!

Nadia's book, " Dreaming to Done" is an incredible guide straight to your soul's journey and to your heart. As I read more and more, I could feel such a profound soothing of her words as if I was being held and loved the entire time. So many truths that everyone can relate to and depth that can truly be captured by those like me who have a huge conviction to staying true to my soul's dreams and mission on this planet. I know where to turn to, when I need an energetic hug!

- Ellie Laliberté, Award Winning Author of Letters From You to You, Self-Awareness Coach

So refreshing!

If you've ever stared at a half-finished vision board while eating cold pizza and thought, "Wow, I'm crushing life," this book is your wake-up call. Nadia doesn't just make you dream bigger, she shows you how to actually finish the thing. It feels like a soul workout wrapped in a cozy chat. You'll laugh, you'll nod, and at some point you'll probably mutter, "Fine, Nadia, I'll do it." By the end, you're not just dreaming, you're actually doing.

- Jenn Noble, Relationship Coach, Speak Honest LLC

A masterpiece for self-care!

Without a doubt, this book is LIFE inspiration and whole heart happiness for me. It gives me a delicious ease I've been seeking. Transformative and heart-led, it invites action, self-care, and dream-to-done purpose — with art and doodling that spark joy and deepen embodiment. Highly recommended.

- Shelley A Murdock, Bestselling Author of In Search For Longevity, Longevity Coach

A truly transformative and grounding read!

 I just finished reading From Dreaming to Done and was so touched. Nadia's words held up a mirror, showing me places where I wasn't fully in harmony with my soul's desires. The reflection questions, personal stories, and creative tools helped me see where I'd been hiding from my dreams, while offering practical, spirit-led steps to move forward.

- Tara Preston, Evolutionary Guide for Midlife Mothers & Leaders, Akashic Teacher, Transformational Space Holder

Heartfelt and uplifting!

Dreaming to Done is such a warm and empowering book. Readers are invited to embark on a soulful journey of self-discovery, learning to trust their intuition and embrace their unique path. It's a heartfelt reminder that true success comes from within, offering practical guidance on aligning with one's soul map. An enlightening and uplifting read for anyone ready to follow their heart's desires!

- Heather Colman, Bestselling Author of Our Money Narrative, MBA

Empowering and deeply insightful!

Nadia's book is nothing short of fantastic! Filled with soft guidance and profound teachings to help you build emotional resilience. It beautifully illustrates the journey from breakdowns to breakthroughs, emphasizing the power of inner guidance and emotional root systems. A must-read for anyone seeking to reconnect with their true self and rise above life's storms!

- Danielle C Baker, Bestselling Author of Bringing Up The World, RECE

Filled with clarity and courage!

"I don't help you dream more. I help you finish the dream your soul has never let go of." This is the heartbeat of Nadia's book. From Dreaming to Done is about starting imperfectly, embracing embodiment, and making progress over perfection - because done is better than perfect. With clarity and courage, Nadia shows how to move from circling to completing, from dreaming to living. The results from following her guidance are outstanding. Thank you, Nadia, for this gift - may your readers and your mission flourish as they finish what truly matters.

- René "Impact, Income & Freedom" Baratella, Business Coach

Time to bring your dreams to life!

When our presence fades, our dreams get pushed aside. But they never stop whispering: 'I'm still here.' When you're ready to bring your dreams to life, there's no one better than Nadia to guide you through the portal of creation and find your own finish line. She offers a pathway using art, creativity, and your own soul for birthing your dreams and becoming your true essence. If you have been asking for a guide, Nadia is it. Read this book, take the steps along your path that Nadia describes, and watch your dreams and your life blossom.

- Jennifer Rinehart, Rebel Oracle + Keeper of the Pollinator Codes

This is a Must Read!

What's your dream? I highly recommend "From Dreaming to Done," where Nadia lovingly guides you through her unique process of dream completion. If you have a dream that is sitting on a shelf, "From Dreaming to Done" will help you dust it off and put it into powerful action and successful completion. This is a must read for anyone ready to come into full bloom with their purpose and passion.

- Joy Balma, Bestselling Author of Crack Your Good Girl Code

Good For the Soul!

Nadia's book, From Dreaming to Done, is truly good for the Soul. The conversational style felt as though she was speaking directly to me. It was refreshing to be guided to realize our Soul's purpose within a safe space, without being told that the only way to succeed is to 'grind.' I appreciated the reminder that self-care is vitally important to complete what we are born to do, and I enjoyed the practical exercises and key takeaways to integrate learnings at the end of each chapter. I highly recommend this beautiful heart-led book.

- Lisa Anna Palmer, Founder & CEO, International bestselling author, and podcaster. Co-Founder & Co-Chair of Mustakabali Wetu-Our Future NGO

What a Gift to the world!

Reading From Dreaming to Done felt like sitting across from my sister, hearing her share her heart. Nadia has a gift for putting into words the struggles and hopes so many of us carry, and for showing a way forward that feels gentle but powerful. This book isn't theory. It's lived wisdom, and it speaks to anyone who has ever had a dream they don't want to leave unfinished. I couldn't be prouder of her.

- Nadim Braun, Head of Operations

Dedication

To the Heart Leaders who have inspired, supported, and believed in me — thank you for holding the vision when I could barely see it myself.

To you, dear reader and fellow Heart Leader, about to embark on this *From Dreaming to Done* journey with me: this is for every dreamer who dares to finish what their soul began.

To my younger self and my future self — thank you for your stamina, clarity, perseverance, and unwavering heart to complete what truly matters.

To Eric, my partner in every adventure — thank you for believing in me, in us, and for choosing *us* through every season. You have made our shared life a dream worth living. My gratitude to the one who walks beside me, in sunshine and in shadow, always returning to the choice of us.

To Laura Hollick and the Soul Art® Certification training that has shaped me, and for her encouragement to step more fully into my own creative identity while honoring the roots I've received from Soul Art®

And to the Divine — for guiding my hands, my heart, and my path — and to all the hearts who walk alongside me, now and always.

My Dream

I dream of a world where heart-led women win big not just for themselves, but for the good they can do when they rise.

I am here to turn dreamers into finishers, guiding them to complete the visions their soul began, so their work can circulate wealth, love, and change in the world.

Through the sacred weaving of art, healing, and business, I help women embody their essence, align with their deepest truth, and build the structures that allow their dreams to flourish.

Because when we finish what we were born to do, we don't just transform our own lives; we ignite a ripple of generosity, joy, and impact that outlives us.

"I don't help you dream more. I help you finish the dream your soul has never let go of."

— *Nadia S. Krauss*

PREFACE

"An empty lantern provides no light.
Self-care is the fuel that allows your light to shine
brightly." — Author Unknown

What if self-care was the highest form of manifesting and self-actualizing your dream?

Hello, brilliant heart and beautiful Soul. I'm so glad you found your way here, reading these pages. I began writing this book with that quote and this question because not taking exquisite care of myself was the reason I kept circling my truest dream, what I was born to do, for far too long.

This is the first spark of the **Soul Map Spiral Process**™ — what I call the **Dreamspark**. Every dream begins with a flicker, a yearning that lights up from within.

It's why every business I started seemed to end in burnout. Each burnout wasn't the end, but part of my Spiral — inviting me to go deeper and returning me again and again to that original spark until I finally learned how to nurture it.

You see, I knew how to be everything for everyone else. I was skilled at using my highly sensitive perception to attune to my environment and meet others' needs. I excelled at people-pleasing, at the cost of my own peace and fulfillment. I had no boundaries, and as long as everyone else was happy, I believed I was too.

For years, decades even, I peeled back the layers of co-dependency, enmeshment, and overgiving, all while being a high-achieving, Type A personality and a naturally born leader. I know you can relate, because you are, too.

I know you are deeply feeling. Like me, you've experienced a lot, emotionally, spiritually, and professionally. You are not a beginner when it comes to soul exploration.

Deep inside you lives a dream, a vision you've never quite let go of, yet one you've never fully brought to completion. You find yourself in a space of inner transition: ready for more, yet tired of push energy, depleted by systemic structures, and weary from the pressure to perform.

You are a soulful leader, intuitive, resilient, and quietly powerful. You've been the strong one for others, and now you are learning that softness isn't weakness; it's a deeper kind of strength. This next chapter isn't about proving your power. It's about embodying it, fully and gently.

I wrote this book for you.For me. And for all of us, highly energetically sensitive souls who stepped into high-achieving, high-performing roles just to feel like we belonged.

I wrote this book because, just like you, I refuse to leave my dream unfinished.

And because I believe, just like you, that my heart and soul came into this body and world to *win big and do good*.

We are living at a crucial turning point in human evolution. It's clear we face challenges we can no longer avoid. We will either rise to the occasion or succumb to self-destructive patterns. I know I'm here to rise, and now I'm showing others how to rise, too.

I'm showing up with big dreams to change the world, one brilliant heart and beautiful soul at a time, because:

I've lived the in-between:

The fire of the vision and the stillness of the stall.

I know the ache of circling the same soul dream for years.

And I've found the pathway to finish what truly matters, so we all can win big and do good, becoming the change we wish to see.

This book is a **Soul Map Spiral™** process and a sacred permission slip.

Not just for creatives. But for anyone whose dream still whispers, *Don't forget me.* Through these pages, I'll walk you through the 7 layers of the Spiral — from the first spark of a dream to the deep integration of living it fully.

With this book, you're entering a portal to discover your magic.

From dreaming to done.

From delay to devotion.

From fear to full embodiment.

Because I know:
You didn't come this far to leave your dream unfinished.

From one dreamer to another,
It's time to finish what you were born to do.

Big love,
Nadia

As you turn the page into the Introduction, notice how this book begins to shift from my personal story into your Soul Map.

Here, you'll see how the Soul Map Spiral™ process becomes the gentle framework guiding you step by step — from spark to completion. Let's walk this path together.

INTRODUCTION

"I don't help you dream more. I help you finish the dream your soul has never let go of."
— *Nadia S. Krauss*

This book is a safe space where your depth is not seen as a weakness, but as a gift. It's structured without pressure. A gentle container for your creative flow.

A companion and guide to help you authentically complete your Soul's vision.

It offers support to activate safety in your nervous system for expansion.

It provides *reminders* instead of motivation, a return to what you've always known deep inside.

This book does not skim the surface. It won't push you to act out of alignment with your true nature. It's not about lofty spiritual concepts without grounded implementation. It's not a path that will activate stress, force, or grinding energy in your body. It will not leave you feeling lost in the noise of life or stuck in unproductive loops. Quite the opposite.

It offers *gentle leadership*, not hyped-up hyperbole.

It activates *body intelligence*, not just mental processing.

It guides you through sacred self-care rituals, infused with rhythm, healing, and repetition. This is a creative field that will not overwhelm you; it will bring you home.

My Role in This Journey

I am not a coach, and I won't tell you what to do.

I am a guide, reminding you of the wisdom you already carry.

The wisdom that forms your Soul Map for finishing what you were born to do.

I help you take that final step:

From *eternal searching* to *sacred completion*.

I bring you back to the dream your soul has never given up on, and help you embody and self-actualize it:

In love.
In aligned action.
In rhythm.
In pause.
In presence.

I don't help you dream more.
I help you finish the dream your soul has never let go of.

This book will guide you through the process of understanding your unique Soul Map framework within the context of:

1. Hearing the Call

2. Initiating the Shift

3. Cultivating the Practice: Honoring the Timing

4. Doing the Work: Trusting Yourself

5. Walking the Talk: Giving Yourself Permission

6. Gentle Courage: Your Dream Fulfilled

7. From Dreaming to Living as Joy in Motion

You are:

- Creative, by nature.

- Whole, by design.

- Powerful, by claim.

- Magic, by heArt.

- Sexy, by an empowered body.

- Talented, by your Soul's gift.

This book and your engagement with it will remind you of that.

Now that you've felt into the essence of this journey, we step onto the spiral itself.

The first layer of the Soul Map Spiral™ process is the Dreamspark — that initial whisper, yearning, or spark that ignites your Soul's call.

Chapter One begins here: hearing the call that awakens the dream within you.

TABLE OF CONTENTS

CHAPTER ONE
Your Dream Is a Soul Map to What Matters Most to You

"Hearing about your Divine potential and your Soul's gift is an entirely different thing than embodying your Divinity by applying your Soul's gift."
— *Nadia Shana Krauss*

Hearing the Call: A Whisper From the Past

I first heard the call at 11 years old. This was my Dreamspark moment, the very first flicker of a Soul dream that would not let go.

Watching my parents, unhappy in themselves and unfulfilled in their relationship, constantly fighting about money, I felt a deep yearning stir inside me. Even though I didn't know exactly how, I *did* know in my bones that I was going to do things differently. I was going to create a legacy filled with meaning, great relationships, and financial well-being.

My parents did the best they could with what they had, I see that now. They often spoke about Divine potential and the importance of contributing one's gifts to the world. But they didn't know how to *apply* their Soul's gifts. They never truly embodied their Divinity in a way that allowed them to win big and do good.

It was heartbreaking to witness. And it led me to make a firm decision. That decision was my Soul Yes — a vow to live differently, to create something new. Not just repeat the same old story. Little did I know, I'd walk a 39-year journey of trial and error, spirals of healing and empowerment, patterns of stalling, and rhythms of breakthrough. It took until I turned 50 to truly understand how to connect with my Soul Map Spiral™ and how to *finish* what I was born to do, and most importantly, how to guide other heart-led dreamers to do the same.

Writing, publishing, and sharing this book with you is a full-circle moment of completion, for my heart, my soul, and for *you*.

You've Heard the Call, Too

You, beautiful dreamer, have heard the call many times, just like I have.

You know there's no turning back. And that's a

good thing.

You carry the frequency of transition within you. You live on the edge of growth spurts, between what *was* and what's *not yet tangible*.

Your outer world may say, "You have everything."

But your inner world whispers, "I'm just functioning."

You are sensitive, often masked.

Spiritual, though you may not call yourself that.

Intelligent, but tired of always thinking.

Present for those who count on you, yet absent within yourself.

You long for something you can barely name: *Security in the midst of your own depth.* [This is where the Spiral Step In begins: choosing to listen to the ache of your Soul instead of ignoring it.] You no longer want to just "know"; you want to *become*. Not the "next version of yourself," but your true *essence*.

You are not a beginner. You are a soul traveler.

And you are also tired, deeply tired.

What you need isn't a kickstart.

What you need is *you*, as a haven of peace, as a mirror, as a reconnection.

The Challenge: Staying With the Dream

Across these 39 years of coming into my own and finishing what I was born to do, I've often been tempted to give up, sometimes inwardly, sometimes outwardly, and sometimes both.

But I stayed. Because my heart and soul wouldn't let go of the dream. [This is the work of the Preservation Chamber — staying with the dream even when it feels fragile, protecting it until it can grow.] I stayed as true to myself as I could be in each moment, in my body, one stepping stone at a time, each bringing me closer to my vision. That was no accident. That was *gentle courage in motion.*

Let me guide you through short 10-30 minute creative processes to help you cultivate this same staying power. What I call *emotional resilience.*

The Mirror Is You:

1. Where in your body do you carry the energy of the dream that keeps calling you but has not yet been completed by you?

➤ Do you feel it as pressure in your chest? As a longing in your heart? As restlessness in your back?

The answer to this question shifts the dream from "project" to embodied truth.

If you would like to receive a guided meditation and visualization of this 3-question process to help you remember that this dream lives within you to be carried to term through you, you can go here to receive a Soul Map Gift.

https://bit.ly/SoulMapGift

"You don't have to invent your path to finishing the dream — you can just receive it. Right now." - Nadia Shana Krauss

2. What has your intuition been trying to tell you for months that your head keeps

putting off?

➤ Is there a clear yes that you are minimizing? A truth that you've known for a long time?

This question is about the stop sign for self-sabotage. This guided presence process doesn't ask: What do you think you can do? It asks: "What are you ready to receive now?

3. If your dream were your body, what would it ask you to do today?

➤ Listen? Create space? Take a small courageous step?

[This is your Alignment Checkpoint — where you pause, listen, and realign your choices with your dream's wisdom.]

The answer to this question puts an end to overthinking. It brings manifestation into the moment — not with to-do lists, but with present embodiment.

My Soul signature in writing this book and guiding you through the From Dreaming to Done Journey is this:

"If mindset is king, then embodiment is queen, and you don't have to push your dream. You get to inhabit it." - Nadia S. Krauss

[This is the Expression Gate opening: where what once lived as thought becomes embodied action, visible in your life.]

It has worked for me. It can work for you. And it most certainly has worked for others.

Testimonial/ Case Study:
A Journey of Clarity, Transformation & Deep Connection

"I was feeling a lack of direction and encountering blocks to my progress. Clarity was elusive, and I was working far too hard without seeing the results I desired.

Having been immersed in the Energy World for over three decades, it's rare for me to encounter something truly new. However, the Soul Realignment® reading and process introduced me to a fresh, transformative energy. Nadia's magic, combined with her well-crafted and intentional steps, made me feel safe, seen, heard, and understood at a profound level. Her compassionate nature and eloquent way with words allowed me to perceive aspects of myself that had long been hidden.

The results were extraordinary. I gained so much more clarity, serendipity, and lightness. Burdens were lifted, and powerful mantras were created that keep me aligned, help me remember my Essence, and attract what I truly desire with increased confidence and peace.

Nadia, YOU are the magic and the medicine. Your way with words, your gifts, and your process have truly deepened my love for myself and humanity. I love you!

To anyone considering this journey, know that the gentle and profound transformation offered by Nadia's process is like providing your Essence with the nourishment it needs to flourish." - Christina Courtwright Jenkins, U.S.

What echoes in you from her story?

Christina's results reflect the power of Done / Integration — where the spiral comes full circle and a new wholeness is lived.

Chapter Recap

To walk with the dream your Heart & Soul still hold

1. **The Awakening: A Vow to Live Differently**
   A sacred seed was planted in childhood —
   a vow born not from rebellion, but from
   remembrance. You knew, even then, that you
   were here to do life differently: with depth,
   devotion, and divine meaning.

2. **The Spiral Path: Becoming Takes Time**
   Your dream did not unfold in a straight
   line. It spiraled through decades of growth,
   unraveling, healing, and return. Completion
   is not about speed — it is the soul's slow
   devotion to what truly matters.

3. **The Threshold: Between Who You Were
   and Who You're Becoming**
   This book — your mirror — is here now. You
   are welcome as you are. Masked, sensitive,
   and weary. Within you the ache of sacred
   longing, a pulse of purpose, a truth too
   vibrant to ignore. This is the place where
   magic begins.

4. **The Medicine: Staying With the Dream**
   In a world of hustle, you can choose presence.
   Your medicine is emotional intelligence,

gentleness, and the art of staying. This is what finishes the dream — not force, but fidelity to your Soul's whisper.

5. **The Embodiment: Making the Invisible Visible**
Through Soul Art®, the dream speaks in symbols, colors, and truth. This is how you remember. This is how I returned to myself. Now I offer you, the reader, this same pathway — a mirror, a map, a movement back to your true nature. Home.

Soul Map Ritual - A Spiral to Come Home to Yourself
A Guided Inquiry

Take a moment to pause.
Close your eyes.
Feel your breath enter your body like a sacred guest.

Let this question land softly in your heart:
Where am I on my Soul Map right now?

There is no right answer. Only resonance.

Gently read each milestone again and notice:
* Which one stirs you?
* Which one feels like home?

* Which one feels like a stretch you're ready for?

Now place your hands on your heart or
womb-space and ask:
What do I need to trust this part of the path?

Breathe.
Listen.
Write what arrives below:

I am here: _____

My message from this place: _____

My next loving step: _____

Return to this ritual any time you feel lost
or unsure.
Your Soul always knows the way.

The Soul Map Spiral™

A visual portal to locate your journey

Imagine a spiral path moving from the outer
rim toward the luminous center — each ring
representing a stage of your heroine's journey.

THE SOUL MAP SPIRAL

The Soul Seed
is Stirred

Milestone 2
The Spiral Begins –
You Say Yes

Milestone 3
Threshold Initiation –
You Burn the Old

Milestone 4
Sacred Endurance –
You Stay With the Dream

Milestone 5
Embodied Completion –
You Become the Work

Mark the place that feels most alive to you right now.

Let the spiral show you what is ripening, what is resting, what is reawakening.

Draw, doodle, write in the margins.

- *What has this reflection shown you?*

- *What sacred step wants to emerge from this place?*

What you've just walked through is the rhythm of the Soul Map Spiral™ Process — from Dreamspark to Integration. You'll see these layers woven throughout this book as guideposts on your own journey.

"Every spiral contains its own rhythm of becoming. Trust yours."
— Nadia Shana Krauss

CHAPTER TWO
Dream's Manifesto: If Mindset is King, Embodiment is Queen

"Find the clarity and understanding to lift your Spirit without straying into doubtful indecision."
— *Nadia Shana Krauss*

Initiating the Shift: We Are Our Mothers & Fathers

Even though my parents did the best they could, planting grand visions of winning big and doing good in my young mind, they could only work with what they had. As humans, we often inherit patterns that hurt our true nature. The parents or caregivers who instilled these patterns in us did so because society had instilled them in them.

My parents were big on "thinking the right way," reading books like *The Power of Your Subconscious Mind* by Joseph Murphy or *Mind Power* by John Kehoe. They believed that if they just thought the right way, all their dreams and wishes would come true.

For a long time, I believed it too. If I just thought clearly enough, dreamed big enough, visualized hard enough, everything would fall into place.

But something was missing. [This was my Dreamspark moment — realizing the old story wasn't enough and that something deeper was calling.] It wasn't that my mindset was wrong. It just wasn't the whole picture.

I had learned how to think, but I didn't know how to stay in my body. [Here begins my Soul Yes — choosing to turn inward, to trust my body as a sacred home of wisdom.] I didn't know how to feel difficult feelings without abandoning myself. I hadn't yet learned to trust that my somatic experiences weren't obstacles, but information. That my body was the missing piece. The sacred home of my subconscious. The temple where my wisdom was waiting.

My parents were never taught how to feel and express their emotions. So they dissociated from their bodies when difficult situations arose. I learned to do the same. We are our mothers and our fathers until we do the work of reparenting ourselves and our nervous systems. [This was me stepping fully into the Spiral Step In — breaking ancestral patterns and daring to write a new story.] The work of detecting and transforming survival patterns and coping mechanisms that no longer serve us is what initiates *the shift*. A shift into healing and empowerment, for ourselves, and for our ancestral line.

This is generational healing for the mother and father wound. A sacred line drawn in the sand that begins a new story, for us, our loved ones, our families, and the world. This shift, from what people expect of us and the behaviors we've learned to comply with, is the powerful doorway to positive change. It opens us to the dream that already lives inside us. The Soul's calling that keeps calling.

The path we are meant to walk in this lifetime.

And when I learned how to step into my body and *stay*, something repositioned itself. It *clicked*. I didn't just understand energy shifts conceptually anymore.

I could *feel* the way forward, from the present version of me into the one already living the dream my Soul chose.

A Heavenly Invitation: Embodiment

This chapter is a royal invitation, not just to think

about your dream, but to *feel* it, *move* it, *wear* it, and *become* it. [This is the Preservation Chamber — where the dream is kept alive by embodiment, no longer just an idea but a felt reality.] While mindset, your thoughts, beliefs, and clarity, may initiate the dream, its embodiment, the felt, lived expression, is what rules the realm of manifestation.

A Dream Manifesto is a soulful declaration, a bold, heart-rooted articulation of your deepest desires, visions, and values. It's not a business plan. It's not a goal list. It is a *living document of truth*, speaking from the future-you who already embodies the dream.

A Dream Manifesto is a poetic proclamation of your Soul's vision made visible.

It declares not only *what* you are creating, but *why* it matters, *who* you must become to live it, and *how* the world is transformed by your courageous devotion to it.

The Mirror Is You: Key Elements of a Dream Manifesto

1. Soul Vision

   ° What do you long to *create,*

---

experience, express?

- ○ What dream wants to be lived through you?

2. Sacred Why

- ○ Why does this dream matter — to you and to the world?

- ○ What's at stake if you don't follow it?

3. Embodied Identity

- ○ Who are you becoming through this dream?

- ○ What truth does it call you to live fully?

4. Values + Vows

- ○ What non-negotiables do you stand for?

- ○ What promises are you making to your dream and your path?

[This is an Alignment Checkpoint — the place where you pause, declare your truth, and align your dream with your body and values.]

Testimonial / Case Study
From Feeling Anxious to Energized & Motivated

"Before my Soul HeArt Journey Session, I felt very tired. A little stressed and tense, something that easily happens before an appointment. A kind of anxiety. I also felt a bit confused about the place I found myself in.

Through the process, and during the Soul HeArt Journey Process, I noticed myself becoming calmer and clearer.

I received such good guidance and support on what to expect from the journey which really put me at ease. The explanation of the journey we were about to embark on helped me see more easily the overall picture of our conversation.

After the session, I felt much more energetic and motivated to continue taking action on my own behalf.

Together with Nadia, I came up with a good power statement as an anchor. I loved receiving my Soul Power Mantra through this journey. " – Aina from Norway.

What echoes in you from her story?

[Aina's journey is an Expression Gate —
stepping into her power statement and
mantra, embodying her dream in language
and energy.]

10 Steps to Your Dream's Manifesto

To walk with the dream your Heart & Soul still hold

- We inherited stories around productivity,
  performance, and "pushing through." Realizing
  they are no longer sustainable on the path of
  Soul-led living initiates the shift.

- A pivotal repositioning occurs when you see
  that **embodiment** — not just mindset — is
  what allows true healing and dreaming true-
  to-you to begin.

- We break an ancestral pattern by choosing to
  stay present with our emotions rather than
  dissociating or spiritually bypassing.

- The body becomes a sacred space — not
  something to overcome, but something
  to *inhabit*.

- Your dreams live not only in your vision, but

also in your nervous system — and your nervous system needs tenderness, rhythm, safety and trust.

- The dream is not a place we go to escape the body, but it is the path we walk with the empowered body.

- A heavenly invitation arrives, guiding you inward — offering clarity, not from logic, but from deeper knowing.

- You begin defining your **Dream Manifesto** — a declaration of values, rhythm, and integrity, not just outcomes.

- You recognize that who you become in the process of dreaming matters just as much as the dream itself.

- This chapter closes with a soul-aligned YES — not to doing more, but to being more *you*.

[This is the **Done / Integration** moment — not a finish line, but the lived reality of being more you.]

Dream Manifesto Ritual: A Body Wisdom Activation

1. Create your own Dream Manifesto using the elements of Soul Vision, Sacred Why,

Embodied Identity, Your Values, and Your Heartfelt Vow).

Start with:

"I am becoming the woman who _____."

Complete this in free-form flow. I encourage you to capture symbols that are showing themselves in your heart space or mind's eye. Let colors emerge too.

2. Body Wisdom Activation

A simple, somatic ritual to help you feel into your body and activate your body wisdom:

- Light a candle.

- Place one hand on your heart, the other on your lower belly.

- Allow yourself to drop from your head into your heart and womb.

- Inhale: "I welcome my dream and I will birth it into the world."

- Exhale: "I come home to my body." Now move and activate your body in response to this question: "If your dream could dance, how would it move through you?"

3. Manifesto Collage and Symbols

Now put everything together in a collage. You can sketch symbols, textures, use magazine clippings and colors that represent:

- ° Your heart & soul dream

- ° the version of you already living it

- ° the values you are devoted to carry into this becoming

This will serve as your sacred visual seal that anchors your Dream Manifesto into your body and form.

[Notice how this ritual mirrors the **Soul Map Spiral Process**™ — from the first spark of longing (**Dreamspark**) to declaring your embodied manifesto (**Done / Integration**). This is how we spiral deeper into becoming.]

DREAM MANIFESTO RITUAL

A BODY WISDOM ACTIVATION

1. Create Your Dream Manifesto

I am...

2. Body Wisdom Activation

3. Manifesto Symbol

Your symbol represents your heart and soul dream. The version of you already living it, the values you are devoted to carry into this becoming.

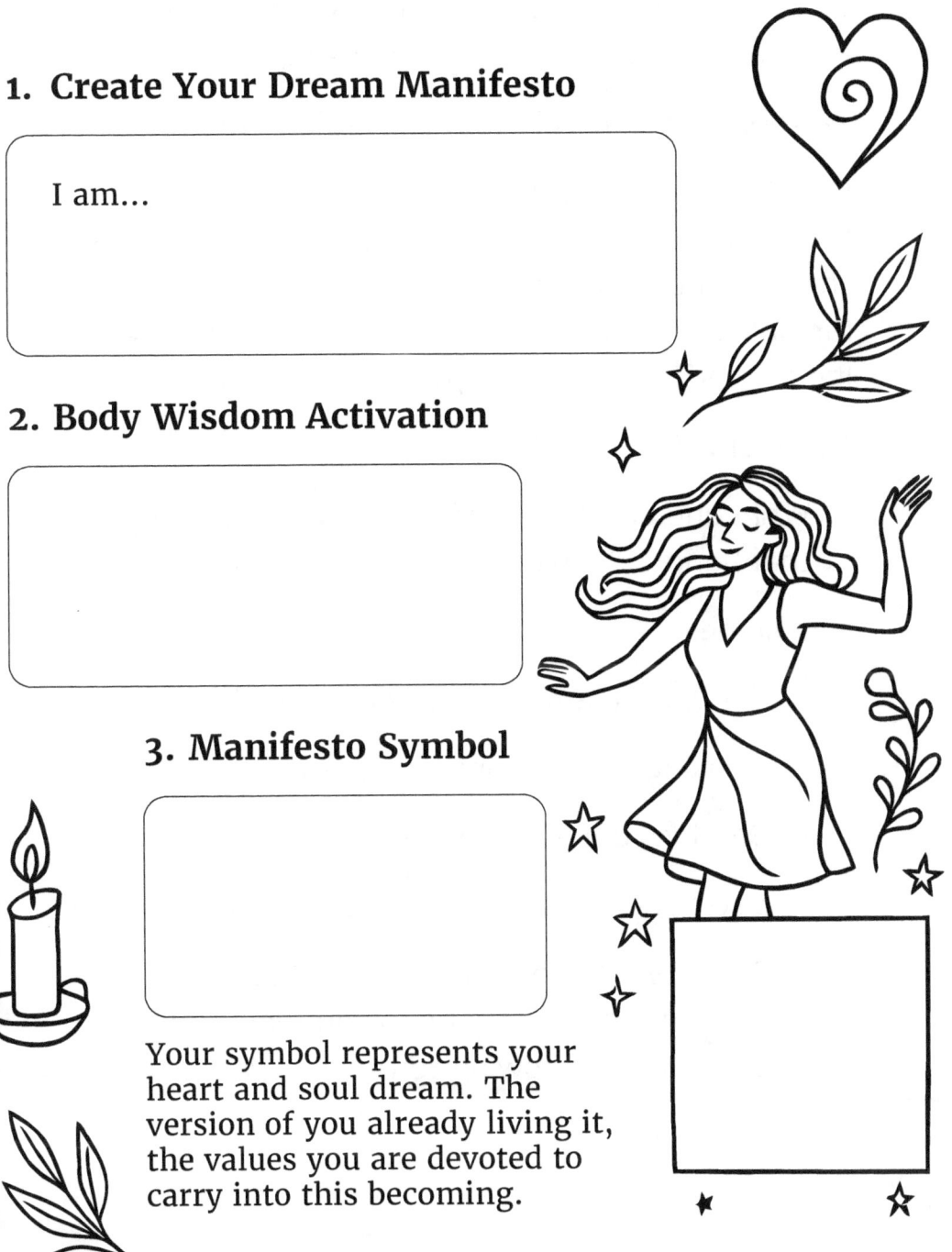

If mindset is king and embodiment is queen, then Spirit Action is their sacred union made manifest. What could be an inspired step that brings your inner alignment into external movement?

Action: Take One Aligned, Embodied Step

Now that your Dream Manifesto is alive within you, sealed with body wisdom and visual truth, take one small, soulful step that brings your dream into the tangible world. This action doesn't have to be grand. It just needs to be true to you.

Ask yourself:

> What one brave, beautiful step can I take today that honors the woman I am becoming?

It could be:

- Sending an email you've been avoiding.

- Booking a space for your dream offering.

- Sharing your Manifesto with a trusted sister.

- Saying no to something that drains your soul.

- Saying yes to something that takes you past your comfort zone to your epic and evolutionary growing zone.

Let your body choose — not your fear.

Let your dream move *you.*

This is not about hustling or striving. It is about listening and honoring.

Let this be the beginning of walking as her: the woman already living her dream.

As you close this chapter, notice where your Dream Manifesto is already alive in your body. You've said your Soul Yes, declared what matters, and felt the shift toward embodiment. This is the Spiral pulling you inward, helping you preserve the sacred spark of your dream. In the next chapter, we step into Sacred Timing — learning why your dream has no expiration date and how each spiral return brings you closer to its fulfillment.

CHAPTER THREE
Sacred Timing: Soul Dreams Have No Expiration Date

"The more you take responsibility for creating and designing your life and soul-aligned livelihood, the more effectively you will be aligning the forces of creation with your desired result." — Nadia Shana Krauss

---

The Dream Begins as a Dancer

The first time I had a dream and followed its call by taking assertive action was when I was 12 years old. I heard the call through a yearning and desire spreading in my heart space.

I want to learn to dance is what the dream said.

At the time, I was living in the city I was born in: Stuttgart, Baden-Württemberg, Germany. I don't quite remember what ignited the yearning and desire. I just remember feeling it intensely in my body.

My body wanted to move in this way. My body wanted to dance, and I wanted to do it well. [This was my Dreamspark, the first flicker of my Soul Map Spiral™ Process.]

Have you ever felt a yearning that didn't begin in your mind — but in your body?

Was there ever a moment when something inside you *knew* you were meant to move, speak, or create in a certain way?

So I looked for dance schools in Stuttgart and found the New York City Dance School in the city center. I told Mum that I was going to do this, asked Dad if he would pay for it, and off I went. [This was my Soul Yes moment — choosing action, however small, to honor the whisper.]

After that, I stretched and practiced dance moves in my room between every one of the jazz dance classes I attended. Until I was 14, I danced at that school.

Then my dad uprooted us, and we moved to Cape Town, South Africa — my mum's birth country. But I kept hearing the call to dance. So I looked for dance schools in Cape Town and tried one, then another, until I eventually swapped dance class for step aerobics and aerobics.

What dreams have you tried to keep alive

through change and upheaval?

Which ones quietly morphed into new forms yet still carried the same essence?

The Red Thread of Desire: Returning Again and Again

At age 18, after living in Cape Town, another dream emerged. I wanted a creative career. I loved fashion and dressing up, so I decided that I wanted to be a fashion designer.

Again, I took action on my dream — figuring out which college I'd go to, how much it would cost, and where I'd work part-time to pay for it. It was clear I wouldn't be able to rely on my father for financial support. Then my dad did it again: uprooted us and moved us back to Germany.

In Germany, I struggled to find my way. I couldn't afford fashion school or living in another city apart from my parents. But I wasn't willing to give up on my dream. So I began an apprenticeship as a dressmaker and started a remote fashion design course to teach me the basics. [Here, the Spiral invited me to step in deeper — letting my dream shift shape without losing its essence.]

After three years of early mornings filled with fashion design aspirations before going to my dressmaking job, I realized I wanted to follow my heart toward another dream — getting married, after dating for two years, and building a life of our own.

Have your dreams ever had to bend and adapt to your reality?

What have you done to keep your desire alive, even when the path shifted underneath you?

I was 18 when I met my partner, 20 when we married, and now, at 50, we are still walking this path together. Not out of habit, but through intention. Every day, we choose each other. Some seasons have been smooth, others stormy, but always, we return to the quiet, powerful act of choosing one another.

When I dreamed of a relationship, I didn't just dream of a marriage. I dreamed of building a life rooted in love, truth, and presence — of being with someone not because I had to, but because I wanted to. That dream lives on, not in grand gestures, but in the daily choosing, again and again, of a shared life forged from soul-aligned commitment.

What relationship or commitment in your life has shaped your ability to stay true to your path?

What have you chosen again and again, even when it wasn't easy?

The Dreaming Never Stops

Getting married so young, I did not give up on dreaming. At 24, I heard another call and felt the yearning of my heart.

But before I tell you about that dream, let me say this: I have always been someone who has dreams and starts things on her own, acting on her own behalf. In Kindergarten, I would invent things to craft. Once, I made a handbag out of paper, glue, and string. I decorated it with paint. My Kindergarten teacher was very impressed, especially when the other kids started asking if I could show them how to make one too.

Just before I started Kindergarten, Mum said at the age of three, was the first time I exclaimed, while moving my body to music: "I am going to be a dancer."

Mum organized ballet classes for me at age 4. At first, I loved them - especially when I was prompted to dance like a leaf in the wind. But when the serious training began, my five-year-old self was scared of the ballet teacher. So Mum didn't force me to continue, and I stopped. Until the call returned at age 12.

Were you a child who dreamed big dreams? What

was your "leaf in the wind" moment?

And when – if ever – did you feel the need to silence that part of yourself?

Dreams are a call to come home to ourselves, to our true nature of gifts and God-given talents. A spiral dance that asks for completion.

The Business Dream: Fitness for Body & Soul

At 24, I decided that I was going to be a business owner. The dream was to open a group fitness studio called *Fitness for Body & Soul* — so I did. I ran that studio for three years, teaching 20 group fitness classes per week on my own, until I burned out. [This was the Preservation Chamber, a pause that felt painful but was sacred protection and a powerful first clue that there is a better way to live dreams.]

That dream taught me that holistic health, wellness, and fitness have always been important to me, core values I hold dearly. It also taught me that I intrinsically knew about the healing effects of the mind-body-heart connection.

Every class ended with a heart and soul relaxation meditation and visualization. The members loved them so much.

Mum told me I wanted to be a dancer at three, and Dad told me that at age ten, when he asked what I wanted to be, I said: "I want to be a healer."

That first self-actualized dream — *Fitness for Body & Soul* — combined both of those truths.

> Which of your early dreams are asking to be fulfilled in new ways now?

> What parts of your life are quietly pointing you back to your natural genius?

Burning the False Path: Letting It All Go

After my first business venture burned me out, I had to take a sabbatical to heal my body. The stress of hustling and my poor eating habits (mostly simple carbs) caused me to gain 40 pounds and develop metabolic syndrome — the precursor to lifestyle diabetes. It was my own need to heal that drove my next dream.

I was going to go back to school to get my Health & Wellness Coaching Diploma — and that I did. I also wanted to be a guide for others on their wellness path. Although it took 11 years for my dream of working as a corporate health coach to materialize, it finally did. Not in Germany but the U.S..

> What healing journey in your life cracked you

open to a new purpose?

What dream was born in the aftermath of a breakdown?

Working three years as a corporate health coach in a toxic work environment was the hardest thing I've ever done. It sucked me dry, killed my spirit, and extinguished my creativity. It took four years to recover. But in those years, I found the essence of this book. I applied it in my own life and career - and now I can share it with you: *From Dreaming to Done – A Soul Map for Finishing What You Were Born to Do.*

Because remember: dreams don't have an expiration date. And what is meant for you by your cosmic design cannot pass you by — especially if you keep taking action on your own behalf.

The Spiral Path: Not Starting Over, Starting Deeper

There is a red thread of your deepest desires, expressed through your talents and gifts — the ones you were born with but need honing. This red thread is also a spiral dance. Following that thread and spiral meant involving my body.

My body had to be part of it — move me, dance me through life, ideally activating healing and guidance in the most creative of ways.

What would it look like to spiral deeper into your gifts instead of chasing a linear path?

What wisdom does your body hold that wants to move your dreams forward?

Becoming the Woman Who Finishes

Back in Germany, I was labeled as idealistic, unrealistic — a "dreamer."

They told me I was too ambitious, that my career interests were too scattered, and that I'd never amount to anything. So I left. Again. Leaving Germany on 11.11.11 was my defiant gesture against those narrow-minded opinions that underestimated the divine potential within us all. [This was my Alignment Checkpoint, the moment I chose my truth over the expectations of others.]

Yes, I'm a dreamer — a Soul Dreamer — who turns vision into reality, step by bold step. My internal guidance is my compass, leading me to manifest what my Soul and Higher Self envision. I am driven by clear values and discernment, guiding others with a moral compass and a commitment to what is true for each individual. I write because teaching and sharing knowledge are my callings. Even when I was working in my group fitness studio was I called to write. Back then it was studio newsletters.

I was sharing my knowledge and teaching about cultivating wholeness in the mind, body, heart & spirit connection, through the fitness classes I taught. It was the first time I created a methodology.

I thought this studio was going to be my life path and steady livelihood. When it wasn't, a diverse career of following my dreams, one dream at a time, followed. And now my diverse career reflects my ability to mentor, support, and lead effectively. It's the reason I do what I do and lead the way I do.

Has it been easy getting to this point in my life? No. It took time. 25 years of dancing the spiral dance. It took ongoing courage to follow my heart, and it is this gentle courage that has the spiral dance come full circle for me at age 50. The year this book and Soul Map was born.

It took emotional resilience, continued clarity, an abundance of stamina, and trust in myself — over and over again. And in that trust came the realization: *Divine timing is always right on time.* I can enjoy the sacred timing of my becoming — and my dreams.

The Mirror Is You: Cultivating the Practice

You've just journeyed with me through my sacred spiral of becoming.

Now I invite you to take a breath, soften, and ask:

What dream is calling you now?

What red thread is tugging at your heart — quietly but insistently?

Where in your life is sacred timing already at work?

Because your Soul Dreams, too, have no expiration date.

And you, too, are becoming — right on time.

The Dream Manifests Through You

There's a moment in the film *Frozen II* when Elsa hears a voice calling her, a voice only she can hear. The lyrics echo the tension I once felt within myself:

I'm afraid of what I'm risking if I follow you...

Into the unknown...

I know what it feels like to resist the whisper. I

know the reality of telling yourself that you are fine when your heart and body are telling you differently. When the mind rationalizes, "But you are successful." After all, I had followed the rules, met expectations, been loved, and accomplished what I thought I should by the standards of others.

But deep within me, there was always a voice. Quiet. Persistent. Soulful.

It wasn't dramatic but it refused to leave. And the longer I ignored it, the heavier life became. It was the voice of my truth. The part of me that knew I was not where I was meant to be, doing the thing I was born for.

This voice is the reason I packed up everything familiar and followed an invisible thread across continents — from Germany to South Africa, back to Germany then the U.S. and now Canada. My chosen home. Yes, there were external moves, but the true journey was inward. Because home isn't just a place. Home is the moment you begin living a life that's truly yours.

The greatest tragedy is not failure. It's living someone else's version of success.

It's building a life that looks good but feels empty. Bronnie Ware, who spent years caring for the dying, captured this ache perfectly in the #1 regret she heard over and over again:

I wish I'd had the courage to live a life true to myself, not the life others expected of me.

I carry this truth like a compass. Now, my dream is not just to live my life fully, but to guide others, like you, to reclaim their dreams, too. To listen to that sacred whisper. To know that it's not your enemy, your distraction, or your undoing. It's your direction. Your power. Your truth. You are not separate from the dream.

The dream manifests through you. You don't have to be fearless. But you do have to be honest. And that first act of honesty, that first yes, is the doorway to everything.

Testimonial/Case Study
From Depleted to Meaning and Joy!

"Before the recent Soul HeArt Journey Session with Nadia ... it was a Tuesday and, to be honest, I have been dealing with some personal issues that have left me depleted at times. I wasn't looking forward to working on Wednesday and Thursday. But I WAS looking forward to engaging with Nadia because we always connect and "dance the dance" together so beautifully.

I didn't really know what to expect from the Soul HeArt Journey Session and I assumed it would be just informative more than anything. Nadia and I have worked one-on-one for 16 months in a comprehensive program and I expected this would be more like a chat session than what our previous work had been, which was more in-depth.

I couldn't have been more wrong about that! Nadia doesn't do anything halfway and it actually turned out to be enlightening and transformative on a deep level which is saying a lot given the amount of soul and personal work we've done together over the years. I always take notes during the session because we come up with such great, useful nuggets of insight. As it turns out, this particular session was so engaging for me!

It was interactive and I felt understood and heard. Not only that, Nadia's intuition is so finely attuned that she connected the dots and even added MORE dots. I have to say that it was an extremely enjoyable and meaningful conversation and session.

After the session, Nadia went above and beyond, creating audio for my use as well as beautiful graphics using the custom affirmations that we created just for me, and for my current life situation and needs. I really use these tools in my life, and I felt so gifted by all of this! I'm very happy with this journey I am on with Nadia and her community of friends."

- With deep gratitude, Leesa.

What echoes in you from her story?

10 Milestones of Your Spiral Dance

To walk with the dream your Heart & Soul still hold

These are not steps to success, but soul markers — sacred milestones on your spiral path. They remind you that your dream is alive, evolving with you.

1. **You remembered joy.**
   Thinking of your earliest childhood memory that involves joy and a natural genius is your soul's memory of your gifts and talents. Remember how allowing yourself to live this joy will anchor this truth of yours in the world, through presence and embodiment.

2. **You said yes to yourself.**
   Remember the first time you said yes to yourself and followed your own desire, and all the times after. You learned the power of listening to your heart and soul and taking aligned action.

3. **You let the dream change form.**
   Your dream whispered through the yearning of your heart and each version of your dream an invitation to return to your essence.

4. **You chose love and sovereignty.**
   Keep choosing you and your dream. Not out of obligation, but devotion and self-love.

5. **You helped others heal.**
   Your work this far has helped so many people. Your dreams serve others while showing you how to care for yourself. Your dream is a total circulation of love that includes you in it.

6. **You met the fire of burnout.**
   When you perform your dream for others you burn out. Burnout teaches you to claim your dream *with* your body, not against it.

7. **You redefined success.**
   The spiral taught you that what looks like failure is often deepening. You reframed the

term "starting over" and realized it's about going deeper and truer.

8. **You left what was familiar.**
   Walking away from the circumstances, people, and things that drain you is your soul's exhale — a courageous step into the unknown where your truest dreams can breathe and blossom.

9. **You saw the throughline.**
   Looking back, you see your dream has never left you. You are always becoming the woman who can live it fully — wild and free.

10. **You now walk with your dream.**
   Today, this book is showing you that there is no need to chase your dream when you can just *embody* it. One milestone on your Soul Map at a time. The framework I share in this book leads you not from theory, but from lived experience — the soul truth I lived and loved into being.

Soul-Aligned Action: Your Sacred Step

Your dream doesn't require a grand gesture; it asks for your presence and your next aligned step.

What's your next sacred step?

Think of the one small, powerful action that honors the biggest insight you gained from this chapter.

Commit with Soul Clarity:

- **I will...** *(name your spirit action)*

- **I will begin on...** *(specific date or moment)*

- **I will complete it by...** *(set a soul-honoring timeframe)*

Let this be a sacred promise, not to perform, but to participate.

Not to prove, but to align. Your dream is already walking with you.

This step simply lets it take root, here and now, one sacred step at a time.

As you close this chapter, notice how your dreams may have changed form, paused, or spiraled back again. That doesn't mean they're gone — it means they're alive, waiting in sacred timing. You've now experienced the Preservation Chamber: where slowing down, healing, and pausing protect the spark so it can grow stronger. In the next chapter, we arrive at the Alignment Checkpoint — the place where you'll learn to discern what is truly yours from what the world expects, so your path becomes clearer and lighter.

CHAPTER FOUR
Staying Power Is
Emotional Resilience

"The future belongs to those who believe in the beauty of their dreams." — *Eleanor Roosevelt*

In the context of this book which is rooted in the spiral path of soul dreams, embodying our gifts, and transformation, emotional resilience is not about bouncing back to who you were before the storm.

It is about growing through the emotional terrain of your From Dreaming to Done Journey. It is the sacred capacity to feel deeply without drowning, stay connected to your dream even when everything is unraveling, trust your timing even when you feel behind, and let grief, burnout, or disappointment shape you into deeper devotion — not disconnection.

It's about returning to your truth when the world

tries to rewrite it, reclaiming your desire after it's been buried by duty, performance, or fear. Letting the spiral deepen you instead of seeing change as failure, and choosing again — your dream, your joy, your self — without apology.

It's not about avoiding breakdowns. It's about allowing breakdowns to become breakthroughs. It's the emotional *root system* that allows your dream to rise again and again, no matter the season.

Cultivating Emotional Resilience With Inner Guidance

This book is not about adding to the already large amount of noise existing in the world, telling you who you are supposed to be in the eyes of others' expectation. This book is not about following trends because everyone else is. It's also not about promoting "busy," "complex," or "working hard" in order to look successful in the sense of what society has deemed the norm. This book is not about spending hours and hours of your life with things that, in the end, do not matter.

What this book is about is reconnecting you to your inherent power, heart, and soul. Finding answers through your inner guidance system and deconditioning everything that someone has taught you that takes you away from that power. It's about cultivating emotional resilience to finish what you were born to do by showing you how you can — chapter by chapter — reconnect to your Soul Map through the magic of creative expression, rebuilding severed channels of intuition and clarity. Opening your channels up to being in tuition by your higher self, your heart and soul, so you can take aligned action on your behalf and dreams.

My Biggest Challenge In Life: The Gift That Feels Like A Curse

Growing up in Germany, I remember the rigidity and skeptical nature of that culture and its people. "I believe it when I see it" is a very common thought form and belief system born out of that same rigidity and skepticism. I remember the fearful and skeptical looks from people when I shared that I was going to open my own business, Fitness for Body & Soul. I remember the look and the pat on my shoulder I got with the words: "Well, good luck with that." I also remember looks of admiration, but they weren't mixed with confidence; rather, I could see fear and doubt.

Today I know that these looks and gestures said so much more about the other person than me. But back then it stung. It hurt and it stayed with me. Then the accumulation of those words, gestures, and belief systems, coupled with my own "failures," shifted something in me. I started to believe them. I started to think of myself as a failure. When I left Germany on 11.11.11 to prove myself and "them" wrong. That's when I had to cultivate emotional resilience through inner guidance to grow my staying power.

[This was the Preservation Chamber — a painful pause that taught me how resilience protects and restores the spark.]

That's when I had to expand my sacred capacity to:

- Feel deeply *without drowning.*

- Stay connected to my dream *even when everything is unraveling.*

- Trust my timing *even when I feel behind.*

- Let grief, burnout, or disappointment shape me into deeper devotion, curing the disconnection.

[This was my Alignment Checkpoint — learning to trust my own compass instead of external projections.]

That's when a deconditioning process began and a honing of my soul gifts and talents. That's when I had to find ways to:

- Return to my truth when the world tried to rewrite it.

- Reclaim my desire after it's been buried by duty, performance, and the fear of not belonging to the "success club" of the world.

- Let the spiral deepen me instead of seeing my past in Germany as failure.

- Choosing again — my dream(s), my joy, my true self — unapologetically.

[This became an Expression Gate — my unapologetic return to what I desired most.]

It's when I learned that my breakdown was a death of an identity that did not truly hold the bigness and capacity of my soul gifts and talents. It's when I learned how to stay within breakdowns and stopped avoiding them. I developed staying power, and with my emotional resilience, I was able to witness The Magic of Transformation over and over again, realizing how allowing my breakdowns became the rise into my breakthroughs. It was this gain of wisdom acquired through lived experience that grounded me deep into an emotional *root system* that allows my dream(s) to rise again and again, no matter the season.

Doing the Work: Trusting Yourself

You, my friend, might be a Time Bender. Used to finding the fastest, most effective way to do things. A hybrid Type, like me, part Activator, part Alchemist.

Like the Alchemist, you are designed to learn and achieve mastery over the physical plane. Your life is a series of learning adventures. These adventures do have a tendency to wear you down, though, if emotional resiliency isn't cultivated.

Through practice, exploration, experience, and learning to trust your gut to follow what feels right and aligned, while allowing yourself to feel difficult feelings, you are designed to delight in your learning.

You need work that feels good and important to you. When you're engaged with work that is fulfilling, you tap into a quality of life force energy that is enduring and gives you energy, momentum, joy, and the feeling of being fully alive.

Like the Activator you are, when you find the work that delights you, you can leap into it quickly, following your inner timing and alignment. You have an internal, non-verbal creative flow that often makes it hard for you to explain what you're doing to others. This is when you are most vulnerable to the projections of others, and if you don't learn how to tend to your emotional housekeeping, you are prone to taking on those projections and belief systems people have about you (that aren't true to begin with).

You have a tendency to do more than one thing at a time, and as a highly sensitive heart and very creative soul, this is correct for you, even though you've probably been told to pick one thing and focus on all of your life. (Remember those projections I was just talking about?)

You also have a tendency to skip steps. That's okay! This is part of you finding the fastest path. Sometimes you have to go back and "fix" steps you skipped. although it is more about a "going deeper." It doesn't mean you screwed up or that you are a failure!

Doing the work and trusting yourself when the shadow shows up takes emotional resilience, the capacity to stay with difficult situations by allowing yourself to feel.

It might not be uncommon that you explode with frustration and anger when you can feel that your energy could be used in fulfilling your purpose, but you don't remember how to engage with direction, leaving you "all revved up" with nowhere to go. Or you might shut yourself down by binging on simple carbs to medicate the pain and make that "revved upness" go numb.

You might feel so much energy in your body when you are all "revved up" that you have a vast amount of "backup" energy. You then can be prone to pushing against your inner flow and inner guidance in an attempt to speed up and control the outer unfolding, leaving you feeling profoundly unfulfilled. Possibly this perpetuates a "crash and burn" pattern of burnout.

I am here to tell you that there is a way for you, a unique way of being in the world that minimizes friction and helps you live more effectively so you can avoid burnout. You have an inner compass called your Sacral (second chakra) that lets you know when an opportunity feels right. It's literally where the term "I know it in my gut" comes from because many of us feel intuition as somatic hits in our body. Basically, what I am saying is that you're designed to follow what feels good, but very often you have to re-learn how to trust that inner feeling.

Your logical mind and cultural conditioning often have trained you to ignore this vital inner compass. Your Sacral works best when you wait to see what shows up in your life and then allow yourself to follow the things that feel good. It can feel hard to wait to respond because you've been trained to go out and "make it happen" — to perform, push, and grind, all in an attempt to control. It takes a lot of energy to live that way but if you allow yourself to stop for a minute, slow down, take a breath, and listen, you will see what shows up in your life by divine orchestration. You can then allow yourself to "feel" your way into soul alignment. And when you cultivate this practice, you will slowly recover your connection to your powerful inner compass.

Know this: You can allow yourself to slow down once in a while because, once something feels good and aligned and your Sacral says, "go," you move very quickly, often taking quantum leaps over others.

It's important for you, even though it feels unnatural, to take stock of who will be impacted by your choice and make sure you inform them about what you're about to do. Your internal, non-verbal creative flow can cause you to struggle with translating what you're about to do into words.

Stopping and explaining to someone what you're doing or that you don't need help can cause you to lose your connection to your internal non-verbal creative flow. As unnatural as it can seem, when you inform the people about your actions and how it will impact them, it can actually prepare the way for you to follow your creative flow with minimal disruption and drama.

Informing isn't asking permission. You don't need permission. Informing simply allows people to move out of your way and support you so you can take action on your inspirations. Your natural alignment with your inner creative flow ultimately benefits everyone around you.

Testimonies of the Soul Realignment® Power Retrieval Process

Here is one from Leesa, in the U.S.: "I was just thinking about our 16 months of one-on-one. It was the best investment in myself that I've ever made. Looking back. I have so many tools, now. So much confidence in myself. Even when I don't feel confident, at times. Does that even make any sense? I think it does, and you know what I'm saying. You opened my mind, my eyes, and my heart. Thank you."

And another from Evi, in Italy:

"Before my work with Nadia, I felt helplessly overwhelmed and could observe how my reaction to external circumstances was not appropriate to the actual circumstances. I knew intuitively that there were deeper root causes that wanted to come to light.

I find the work with Nadia very pleasant, full of joy, exciting, and insightful. Also full of surprises and powerful insights that I would never have recognized alone.

After our work together, I feel stronger

and more secure, I am calmer and more deliberate, less impulsive. The trust in myself is constantly increasing, I believe in a higher power that means well, accompanies me, and shows me the way when I am ready to see it then this way opens up for me.

I love this feeling of Soul Health Mentoring with Nadia and the 1 to 1 journeying. Being in such close contact with each other and being accompanied on my path. I have done many group training and coaching masterclasses etc. but never allowed myself this 1 to 1 experience. I am extremely grateful to have taken this step now.

I highly recommend the journeys and Soul Health Mentoring with Nadia because I wish everyone had the support to tackle the difficulties and problems that arise in everyday life at the root. Addressing the root and not just scratching the symptoms on the surface creates change."

What echoes in you from these stories?

The Rooted Tree of Emotional Resilience Quiz

What season is your emotional resilience in right now? What sacred roots need tending?

Answer each question by choosing the phrase that resonates most with you **right now**. There are no wrong answers — just doorways to deeper understanding.

ROOT 1: Feel Deeply Without Drowning

When a wave of emotion rises, I usually:

A. ☐ Numb out, distract, or scroll away from it.

B. ☐ Analyze or journal it into control.

C. ☐ Let myself feel it, but secretly wish it would pass faster.

D. ☐ Breathe into it, welcome it like a sacred messenger.

E. ☐ Dance, cry, or create with it until it becomes an offering.

ROOT 2: Stay Connected to Your Dream in Chaos

When life feels like it's unraveling, I:

A. ☐ Abandon my dream until things "calm down."

B. ☐ Question whether I even deserve the dream.

C. ☐ Try to keep pushing forward, but feel disconnected.

D. ☐ Find small ways to stay tethered to my dream.

E. ☐ Deepen my devotion and ask my dream how it wants to evolve.

ROOT 3: Trust Your Timing

When I see others "ahead" of me, I tend to:

A. ☐ Compare and shrink.

B. ☐ Get anxious and speed up.

C. ☐ Doubt my path and pause.

D. ☐ Remind myself I am on soul time.

E. ☐ Celebrate their progress and stay rooted in mine.

ROOT 4: Let Difficulty Deepen You

When grief, burnout, or disappointment show up, I:

A. ☐ Try to fix or "get over it" fast.

B. ☐ Hide it, fearing it will derail everything.

C. ☐ Let it linger, unsure how to alchemize it.

D. ☐ Ask what it wants to teach or transform.

E. ☐ Allow it to initiate me into greater strength

and clarity.

ROOT 5: Return to Your Truth

When others project doubt or disapproval, I usually:

A. ☐ Doubt myself too.

B. ☐ Work harder to prove them wrong.

C. ☐ Feel confused or disconnected.

D. ☐ Turn inward and reconnect to my Soul Map.

E. ☐ Speak, move, or create from the fire of my truth.

ROOT 6: Reclaim Desire

When my true desires whisper, I tend to:

A. ☐ Ignore them — they feel selfish or unrealistic.

B. ☐ Hear them, but don't know what to do with them.

C. ☐ Let myself want things only in secret.

D. ☐ Name them, write them down, honor them.

E. ☐ Move toward them with devotion, no matter how slow.

ROOT 7: Choose Again, Without Apology

When I've fallen off track or shifted course, I:

A. ☐ Feel like I've failed.

B. ☐ Struggle with guilt or regret.

C. ☐ Try to get "back to where I was."

D. ☐ Start again with gentle grace.

E. ☐ Redefine the path entirely and walk forward with power.

The Mirror is You: Now Reflect

Count how many you answered in each category (A, B, C, D, or E).

Most As? You might be in your **Winter** — in need of rest, repair, and reconnection.

Most Bs? You're in **Late Fall** — ready to release old stories but still navigating inner doubt.

Most Cs? You're in **Early Spring** — the roots are forming, and your dream is stirring.

Most Ds? You're in **Full Spring** — aligned, curious, and grounded in inner guidance.

Most Es? You're in your **Soul Summer** — living from your Rooted Tree and expanding with grace.

Sacred Questions to Water Your Roots:

- Which root feels most nourished right now?

- Which one is calling for your attention or love?

- What is one Spirit Action you can commit to this week to strengthen your Rooted Tree?

Top 3 Takeaways: Staying Power Is Emotional Resilience

1. Emotional resilience isn't about "bouncing back" — it's about deepening.
   You don't return to who you were before the storm; you evolve into someone more rooted, real, and ready to hold your dream with greater capacity.

2. Breakdowns are not failures. They are thresholds.
   When honored and felt through, breakdowns become sacred turning points that usher in your next breakthrough and anchor your staying power.

3. You already have an inner compass — your body knows.
   Your Sacral guidance system (your gut feeling) is a powerful ally. Reconnecting to it gives you access to sustainable energy, aligned timing, and soul-aligned momentum.

Chapter Recap

- Emotional resilience is your *root system*, not your armor. It allows your dream to rise again and again, no matter the season.

- Staying power means *feeling deeply without*

drowning, not bypassing or numbing the difficult emotions.

- Trusting your soul's timing (even when others seem "ahead") is part of your sacred path.

- Burnout isn't failure — it's a sign that you've been performing your dream instead of *embodying* it.

- You're allowed to change your mind, start again, and *choose yourself* without apology.

- The spiral of your dream is not linear. What feels like starting over is often just going deeper.

- Your gifts grow through your own healing — you've already helped others by embodying your truth.

- The Rooted Tree of Emotional Resilience helps you assess and tend to your emotional seasons, from Winter (rest) to Soul Summer (expansion).

- Your Sacral Center (gut) is a real-time guidance system; it tells you what's aligned. Learning to trust it is key.

- Cultivating resilience means rewriting inherited stories, breaking cultural conditioning, and remembering that you are not here to perform, but to *create from the soul.*

Soul Map Ritual: "Follow the Gut, Feel the Flow"

In this chapter you've uncovered how your creative energy works best — in alignment with your gut and inner compass, not by pushing or grinding. Now it's time to *experience* that intelligence in your body, not just read about it.

Sacral Response Map: A Dialogue with Your Yes & No

Step 1: Create a two-part Soul Map

On a blank piece of paper, draw a vertical line down the middle.

- On the left side, title it: "My Sacral Yes"

- On the right side, title it: "My Sacral No"

Step 2: Tune into the Body

Close your eyes. Place one hand on your lower belly, just below the navel — your Sacral Center.

Take a few slow breaths and *recall a moment* when you said yes to something that felt deeply aligned. Let your body remember.

Then do the same for a no — a time you *knew*

something was off, even if you didn't speak up.

Step 3: Express it Visually & Viscerally

- Use colors, symbols, shapes, even words or textures to express how your Sacral Yes and No *feel* in your body.

- Let this be intuitive. Don't overthink it. You are mapping your inner compass.

Step 4: Write to Integrate

Below your artwork, answer this in your journal:

"What does my body feel like when I am in alignment with my inner creative flow?

What does it feel like when I override it or betray my own knowing?"

Let the wisdom come from your body, not your head.

Spirit Action: This week, when a new opportunity, idea, or impulse arises, pause.

Ask your gut: "Does this feel good in my body? Does this feel like a Sacral Yes?"

Then, and here's the courageous part, trust it. Even if you can't explain it to others yet. Even if it means waiting. Trust the timing. Trust the knowing.

Then inform those impacted. Not for permission —

but for grace.

As you close this chapter, notice how your own staying power shows up. Every breakdown, burnout, or doubt can become part of your Preservation Chamber — where your dream is held safe until you're ready. You've now experienced the Alignment Checkpoint, where you reclaim your compass and re-choose yourself without apology. In the next chapter, we cross the Expression Gate — where your dream moves out of hiding and begins to take visible form in the world.

CHAPTER 5
The Secret Wake-Up
Call From Love

"Be a full cup of love sharing from her overflow."
— SARK.

From Mess to Message

Why do I call it a "secret" wake-up call from love? Because so often, life sends us events to catch our attention, especially as changemakers, so we can course-correct the path we're on, both individually and collectively.

What looks like a crisis or failure is often a blessing in disguise. [This was me stepping into the Spiral again, where the mess held the seed of the message.] But uncovering the blessing takes work. We have to excavate it, peel back the layers to find the gems it carries. The message is hidden, secret even. And before we can access that message, we usually have to move through a mess.

Maybe you've already had your share of messy wake-up calls from love, the kind that sends you searching for a compassionate sanctuary, hoping to understand what it all means. You were trying to decipher the message behind the mess. And underneath that desire is a deep yearning for reinvention, to find your truest purpose and live from that place.

Maybe you found yourself in an identity crisis, a spiritual awakening, a divorce, and suddenly, your old life no longer fits. But you're not quite sure who you are now, or what's next.

Your energetically sensitive, visionary nature asks you to hone your spiritual gifts. You've already helped so many. Perhaps so many, in fact, that your *own* dream got buried under your success. But that whisper — *Don't forget me* — keeps calling.

Your dream, still alive, wants to show you how your gifts can serve not just others, but *you*, too. When you answer that call, you begin to see that your dream is tied to your creativity, your spiritual nature, your unique way of seeing the world. You are not separate from the dream — the dream manifests through you. As you actualize it, you become part of the total circulation of love.

Maybe another messy wake-up call from love appeared in your relationship, as you longed for your partner to show up more fully. You wanted to meet each other in a deeper place. But here's the truth: we cannot control the choices others make. We can only choose for ourselves.

In my own experience, love invited me to look at my patterns: co-dependency, enmeshment, and people-pleasing, and to examine the lineage of women in my family who may never have felt free or fulfilled in their relationships. As women today, we have access to choices our mothers didn't.

And perhaps your messy wake-up call from love is this:

You're tired of feeling like an empty, depleted cup when you long to be a full vessel of replenishing love, sharing from your overflow, *winning big and doing good*. You're curious about how to build a life grounded in both self-care and soul-care. You want to realize the dream your soul has held for you — and finally live your truest purpose, fully and unapologetically.

The Secret to Finishing Is Unapologetic Self-Love Leadership

My messiest wake-up calls became my greatest

transformations. I wrote about them in my first book, *The Magic of Transformation – Igniting & Manifesting Soul Desires*, a memoir-meets-guidebook for the woman just beginning to awaken to her soul.

She's feeling the pull.

To trust her desires.

To believe that magic might be real — especially *hers*.

From Dreaming to Done is for the woman who's already awake to her soul desires. She's circled her dream long enough. Now, she's ready to finish what she came here to do. Not someday, now. I didn't write this book to wake you up. I wrote it to walk you all the way home, to help you finish the dream.

Let me share with you one of the biggest, messiest, and most painful wake-up calls that changed everything for me and marked the beginning of unapologetic self-love leadership. It was also the beginning of the end of my life in Germany. My new life cost me my old one.

This is the story of my bankruptcy, after giving my third business in Germany everything — to the point of self-sacrifice, self-abandonment, and complete exhaustion. My body collapsed under the weight of what I was carrying.

I still remember the call with a debt collector and how they tried to shame me when I told them I would be filing for bankruptcy.

Before it felt like a wake-up call from love, it felt like a wake-up call from hell.

[This was the Preservation Chamber, when life stripped everything away so I could finally hear what love was saying.]

Germany, for all its strengths — universal health care, free college, paid holidays — was a restrictive environment for me. To access those benefits, you had to follow a narrow path. My father disrupted that path. He moved our family between Germany and South Africa, always trying to outrun his own financial troubles — and passing that instability onto us. I never felt safe. There was no consistency, no steady ground.

I attended four primary schools and five high schools. In my final school year in South Africa, my dad decided to return to Germany *yet again*. I chose to stay behind and finish school, living with friends of the family. But cultural clashes, between a Muslim household and my European upbringing, made it impossible.

I was not willing to be converted or changed. I called

my parents and asked them to buy me a ticket back to Germany. As a result, I never graduated. At 18, I couldn't benefit from the German system. My father had ripped me out of it, and my mother, financially dependent on him, had no say. I worked at McDonald's.

At 20, I got married, only to repeat the same patterns I'd seen growing up. My husband took care of me. He was the provider.

I've always had ambition, drive, and strong will. I wanted to build my own independence. But Germany's systems didn't allow for me to be free or unique. I had been pulled out of the system and couldn't find my way back in. There are benefits to the box, the rules, the structure. Germany is a well-oiled machine. But I didn't benefit from any of it. I became an outlander in my country of origin. I didn't belong.

Now I know: my heart is fierce, independent, and pioneering. Germany was never meant to help me fly. My breakthrough came when my husband and I sold everything we owned and left Germany on 11.11.11 to live and work on a cruise ship. That bold step was the beginning of unapologetic self-love leadership for me. [This was my Alignment Checkpoint — when I chose truth over performance and self-love over sacrifice.]

The first step toward happiness, healing, and a new life. It was the start of rewriting my money story and my career path. Healing one belief, one habit at a time. Learning to let money become a trusted ally while circulating my gifts in the world. Treating abundance as my soul's birthright.

Walking the Talk: Giving Yourself Permission

Over the past 14 years, I've learned to:

- **Live in integrity with money** — spending, saving, and investing in ways that feel aligned with my values instead of fear or pressure.

- **Enhance alignment with more love, joy, success, and wealth** — seeing money as part of a holistic, abundant life rather than a source of stress.

- **Use powerful money intentions and embodiment practices** — setting clear financial desires and pairing them with rituals that root them in my daily choices.

- **Grow into my Wealth Identity** — expanding how I see myself, moving from scarcity or "not enough" into the confident embodiment of someone who thrives.

- **Love money and be grateful for its**

presence — treating money not as taboo or transactional, but as energy that supports my dreams and helps me win big and do good in the world.

- **Have regular money dates** — setting aside time to review my finances with mindfulness, gratitude, and celebration instead of avoidance.

- **Stop complaining about money, taxes, or systems** — shifting from blame or frustration into curiosity, gratitude, and conscious action.

- **Own my role as the creator and artist of my life** — taking responsibility for what I shape, knowing that each choice paints the canvas of my reality.

- **Speak the Abundance Prayer by Tosha Silver** (and my own evolved version) — anchoring my faith in Source and affirming abundance as a natural state of being.

- **Witness the power of my thoughts and emotions** — noticing how my inner world colors my outer experience, choosing awareness over autopilot.

- **Be patient, learning to see the power of patience** — trusting divine timing instead of rushing or forcing outcomes.

- **It is what it is and it takes as long as it takes** — practicing surrender to the natural unfolding of life without judgment or resistance.

- **Let go of fear and doubt** — mine and my ancestors' — releasing inherited patterns and stepping into courage with compassion for those who came before me.

- **Release resentment** — unburdening my heart so that forgiveness and freedom can flow.

- **Practice deep self-love, compassion, and forgiveness** — honoring myself as sacred, offering the same tenderness to myself as I do to others, and embodying wholeness.

Overcoming bankruptcy, in body, mind, heart, spirit, and soul, did not happen overnight. It happened through sacred daily rituals that slowly transformed me into a full cup of love, sharing from her overflow. [This was my Expression Gate — transforming breakdown into breakthrough and turning my mess into my medicine.]

Committing to unapologetic self-love leadership means asking often:

"What would love do?" Sometimes it means saying a firm no: "This far, and no further." Every no I spoke brought me closer to my truest yes. And every yes I honored healed a pattern of self-abandonment.

Finding Your Yes — And the Courage to Speak Your No

Charlie Chaplin's poem, *As I Began to Love Myself*, is said to have been written on his 70th birthday in 1959. These words remain a powerful reminder decades later. We don't need to wait until the end of life to come to these insights. We can choose to live them now, as the change we wish to see in our families, our communities, and our world.

As I began to love myself

I found that anguish and emotional suffering are only warning signs that I was living against my own truth.

Today, I know, this is Authenticity.

As I began to love myself

I understood how much it can offend somebody As I try to force my desires on this person, even though I knew the time was not right, and the person was not ready for it, and even though this person was me.

Today I call this Respect.

As I began to love myself

I stopped craving for a different life, and I could see that everything that surrounded me was inviting me to grow.

Today I call this Maturity.

As I began to love myself

I understood that at any circumstance, I am in the right place at the right time, and everything happens at the exactly right moment. So I could be calm.

Today I call this Self-Confidence.

As I began to love myself

I quit stealing my own time, and I stopped designing huge projects for the future.

Today, I only do what brings me joy and happiness,
Things I love to do and that make my heart cheer,
And I do them in my own way, and in my
own rhythm.
Today I call this Simplicity.

As I began to love myself
I freed myself of anything that is not good for my
health – food, people, things, situations,
And everything that drew me down, and away
from myself.
At first I called this attitude a healthy egoism.
Today I know it is Love of Oneself.

As I began to love myself
I quit trying to always be right, and ever since
I was wrong less of the time.
Today I discovered that it is Modesty.

**As I began to love myself, I refused to go on
living in the past, and worrying about the future.**
Now, I only live for the moment, where everything
is happening.
**Today I live each day, day by day,
and I call it Fulfilment.**

As I began to love myself
I recognized that my mind can disturb me, and it
can make me sick.
But as I connected it to my heart, my mind became

a valuable ally.
Today I call this connection Wisdom of the Heart.

We no longer need to fear arguments,
confrontations or any kind of problems with
ourselves or others.
Even stars collide, and out of their crashing, new
worlds are born.
Today I know: This is Life!

The Mirror Is You: Listening to Your Secret Wake-Up Call from Love

1. What is your current "mess"?
   What feels out of alignment, stuck, or heavy in your life right now? Be honest and specific.

2. If this mess were a messenger from Love, what might it be trying to show you?
   What patterns, truths, or longings is it inviting you to see more clearly?

3. Where have you been abandoning yourself in order to be accepted, productive, or safe?
   Name the places where external validation or overgiving has replaced authentic alignment.

4. What would it mean to lead with

unapologetic self-love right now?
What is one boundary, one truth, or one desire you've been afraid to honor — and what would shift if you *did*?

5. What's your relationship with money revealing about your self-worth?
Where do fear, scarcity, or guilt still drive your decisions — and how could money become your sacred ally?

6. What does your dream want *from you*, not just *for you*?
If your dream were alive and breathing, how would it ask you to show up?

7. What past version of you are you ready to bless and release?
Name the version of yourself you've outgrown — and thank her for what she carried.

Walking the Talk: Living the Medicine

Author of From Dreaming to Done

I've been accessing the Akashic Records since I was 10, long before I knew the name for it. Soul completion has always been my calling.

My journey with soul transformation didn't start with training.

It started with a question in my body — in my heart specifically.

It started with an unshakable knowing that I came here to finish something sacred and help others do the same.

Over the years, I've quantum leaped again and again, not because it was easy, but because I learned how to hold myself in the fire of transformation.

Courageous clarity. Soul stamina. Radical self-honoring.

That's the true magic that brought me from dreaming... to *done*.

Yes, I've trained in powerful modalities : Health & Wellness Coaching Diploma, Soul Realignment®, and Soul Art®certifications, and more. I have had my own share of mentors and support. But what anchors my work is this:

- A lifelong devotion to Soul truth
- The ability to stay with what others bypass
- A sacred architecture that transforms insight into embodiment

When I guide women now, I'm not teaching theory.

I'm walking with them through the very terrain I've crossed again and again - with reverence, creativity, and fierce love.

That's what my book *From Dreaming to Done* is built upon.

It's not just a framework.

It's a lived map.

It's what happens when you stop circling your calling and choose to land it — in your body, your work, your world.

If you're done performing clarity and ready to embody it...

If you're here to finish what you were born to do...

Let's begin.

https://www.happywholesomelife.com/

https://soulhealthmentor.com/

What awakens in you as I share my journey?

Creative Exercise: *Your Spiral of Becoming*

"Trace the sacred path you've walked, from breakdown to breakthrough, and witness the message hidden in the mess."

◇ What it is:

A coloring and mapping activity that invites you to visually represent your unique spiral path of emotional resilience, healing, and becoming.

Instructions:

1. At the spiral's center, write a word or image that represents your current challenge, "mess," or breakdown moment.

2. As you move outward along the spiral, write down key "Soul Markers" or insights you've gained — moments when you chose love, courage, boundaries, or truth.

3. Use color to express emotion at each stage. You might color dark and stormy near the center and lighter or more vibrant as you expand outward.

4. At the outer edge, write a message your Soul now holds — what you know to be true from this journey.

5. Bonus: Add symbols, doodles, affirmations, or even a date to mark this spiral as a milestone.

Why it matters:

This exercise anchors the spiral path as a *living metaphor* for transformation - nonlinear, sacred, cyclical. It also helps you reframe your "mess" as a moment of becoming, not failing. Turning your pain into power and beYOUty.

3 Key Takeaways from "The Secret Wake-Up Call From Love"

1. **Messy moments are secret invitations from Love.**
   Crises and breakdowns are often disguised catalysts for breakthroughs. Love calls us back into alignment through these messes, if we're willing to listen and excavate the deeper message.

2. **Unapologetic self-love leadership is a path to soul freedom.**
   Breaking old patterns of self-abandonment, co-dependency, and external validation leads to a life lived from the overflow, grounded in truth, creativity, and personal power.

3. **Reinvention is both personal and collective.**
   When we courageously answer the wake-up call, we don't just heal ourselves. We model new possibilities for our lineage, our communities, and the world.

Chapter Recap

- **Crisis as Catalyst:** What seems like failure (bankruptcy, relationship endings, identity loss) is often a disguised gift — an invitation to change course and reclaim one's true self.

- **From Mess to Message:** Painful experiences carry hidden insight. When we lean into the discomfort, we uncover clarity, creativity, and direction.

- **You are not separate from your dream:** The dream lives *through* you. When you honor your gifts, you honor the dream — you step into the larger circulation of love.

- **Patterns of the Past:** Early instability, lack of belonging, and inherited limitations shape us, but they don't have to define us. These patterns can be rewritten.

- **Bankruptcy as Breakthrough:** The author's financial collapse marked the end of self-abandonment and the beginning of self-love leadership.

- **Unapologetic Self-Love Leadership:** This is a sacred practice of integrity, boundaries, abundance, and alignment. It requires courage to say no and wisdom to follow your deepest yes.

- **Money as a Sacred Ally:** Shifting from fear and scarcity to daily rituals of gratitude, alignment, and trust can heal financial wounding and unlock flow.

- **Healing Is Daily Devotion:** Transformation doesn't happen overnight; it's cultivated through consistent self-honoring actions.

- **Overflow, Not Depletion:** True service doesn't come from sacrifice, but from sharing love from a place of internal fullness.

- **A New Definition of Love:** As Charlie Chaplin's poem affirms, real love starts from within. Living from this place changes how we relate to life, time, purpose, and truth.

One Simple Soul-Aligned Action For You: Write a Love Letter to Your Dream.

Speak to your dream as if it were alive and listening. Tell it what you now understand, what you're ready to receive, and what you're willing to commit to next. Let your dream write back.

This keeps the dream alive as a dialogue, not a destination, and grounds your next sacred step in devotion, not pressure.

As you close this chapter, notice how life's messes have carried hidden messages for you, too. Maybe your own Alignment Checkpoint is calling — inviting you to choose truth over performance, self-love over self-abandonment. You've now walked through the Expression Gate: where the mess becomes the message and your power rises from overflow. In the next chapter, we'll spiral into Gentle Courage — the soft yet fierce strength that allows your dream to be fulfilled without force.

CHAPTER SIX
Follow Through Is Activating the Mission

"Above all, choose to be the heroine of your life, not the victim." — *Nora Ephron*

At age 11, my dad gifted me my first self-help and personal development book: *You Can If You Think You Can* by Norman Vincent Peale. That was 39 years ago, and to this day, the book is still in print. I remember loving its energy. It spoke about believing in yourself and your dreams and drawing confidence from the resources of your own mind.

The book was rooted in Dr. Peale's philosophy of positive thinking. While that alone wasn't enough to take me from dreaming to done, or to reveal the Soul Map that would help me finish what I was born to do, it did one powerful thing: it taught me to see myself as the creator of my reality at a very young age. It planted the identity of someone who wins in life. And that identity served me well until I was 35.

That was the year I filed for bankruptcy, and my ex-business partner called me a loser. [This was my Preservation Chamber — the painful collapse that asked me to pause, reset, and find my truest path.]

The Drama Triangle

That moment was the first time in my life I truly felt like a loser, like a victim of bullying and name-calling, all because I had spoken a boundary and said no.

In 2022, at age 47, I heard about the *Drama Triangle* from a mentor of mine, Alisha Belluga, an iconic and visionary leader in Germany who built a deeply impactful business with out-of-the-box thinking, making millions. Winning big and doing good in the world

So, what is the Drama Triangle?

The Drama Triangle is a social model, developed by Stephen Karpman, that describes dysfunctional relationships characterized by three recurring roles: Victim, Persecutor, and Rescuer. These roles are not fixed; individuals can switch between them, often unconsciously, within a conflict situation. The triangle highlights how these roles contribute to negative interactions and can hinder personal growth and healthy relationships.

In my words: *It's the soap opera of the unconscious human condition.*

For the first time, I could understand the relationship dynamics that had shaped, and limited, my life and business. I often showed up as the fixer and people-pleaser, wanting transformation for others more than they wanted it for themselves. But when I finally drew a line in the sand and said no, when I set a boundary, people (including clients) would often turn on me. Suddenly, I became the villain, and they acted like the victim.

Now, at age 50, I can clearly see why the four businesses I built were never sustainable or lucrative. How could they be when they were founded on the dysfunction of the Drama Triangle? [This was my Alignment Checkpoint — finally seeing the pattern and choosing to build from truth rather than dysfunction.]

Gentle Courage: Your Dream Fulfilled

It took years of *gentle courage* to heal the loss of my Creator-of-Life identity and to reclaim my self-assurance. What I didn't know when I left Germany on 11.11.11 to pursue happiness, healing, and recovery was that I was stepping through a Scorpio gate of death, transformation, and rebirth.

Gentle courage, one step, one heartbeat, one calling at a time, got me here. [This was my Expression Gate — where follow-through and gentle courage merged into mission.] Fourteen years of it. And *The Magic 3* gave me the clarity, stamina, and perseverance to follow through.

The Magic 3 helped me rebuild the identity of a heroine, someone who creates her life with purpose. Combined with my understanding of the Drama Triangle, I've been able to heal the rift and shift out of victimhood again and again. I now know how to exit dysfunctional dynamics. I am no fixer. I am no victim. And I am certainly not the person to blame for someone else's shortcomings.

I am a creator.

A Medicine Woman's Prayer
By Sheree Bliss Tilsley ©

I will not rescue you.
For you are not powerless.
I will not fix you,
For you are not broken.
I will not heal you,
For I see you, in your wholeness.

I will walk with you through the darkness,
As you remember your light.

What Are The Magic Three?

They are:

1. **Igniting your Soul Desire** —
   over and over again.
   Reminding yourself of the dream that
   whispers, "Don't forget me."

2. **Harnessing your Soul Fire** —
   your lifeforce energy —
   to take aligned, passionate action.

3. **Applying Soul Medicine** —
   stopping every now and then to slow
   down, breathe, and listen.
   Your heart and soul will tell you what
   you need.
   Sometimes you'll need rest. Other times,
   a reevaluation or realignment to your
   deepest values and dreams.

Knowing your Soul Desires leads to ongoing clarity.
When things get foggy, those desires act as a North

Star, clearing the air and guiding you forward. Harnessing your Soul Fire and taking aligned action nourishes consistency. And regularly retreating from the busyness of the world to apply your Soul's Medicine cultivates the deep wisdom of your heart and soul.

This practice leads to an unshakable conviction:

What is meant for you cannot pass you by, especially when you keep taking soul-aligned action.

- Igniting Soul Desires lights the path to crystal-clear clarity.

- Harnessing Soul Fire and acting on behalf of your dreams and values builds consistency.

- Applying Soul Medicine regularly anchors the knowing that you have everything you need — exactly when you need it.

The 9 Chimes of Your Soul to Follow Through

In the German language, there is one word for a heart-centered human: *Herzensmensch*. I am most definitely a *Herzensmensch*, through and through! There is also a one-word expression for an artist of life: *Lebenskünstler*. Interestingly, although the language has single words for these two ways of being — requiring a full sentence in English to describe — I often felt "less than" growing up in Germany because of these innate qualities I was born with. A rational approach was often favored over a heartfelt one, and following your head was often considered superior to following your heart and intuition. As if the heart couldn't be trusted, when in fact, living from the heart is a superpower. It's what allows you to live a life true to yourself, not to the expectations of others.

Trusting myself and loving from the heart is my natural way of being in the world. I am always honest with myself and speak the truth, no matter how uncomfortable it may be. I am courageous, powerful, and strong. While I've often been criticized for this, I've also received feedback on how courageous and strong I am — feedback that used to surprise me until I understood that I had been gifted with an ability to help others become less fearful and more patient. I also have a gift for helping others become more decisive and develop inner clarity.

I'm a transparent person — down-to-earth and pragmatic in my approach. Altruistic at my core. While altruism is commonly defined as a selfless concern for the well-being of others, the word *selfless* is often interpreted as self-sacrifice. That's where I diverge. I believe true altruism doesn't require diminishing yourself. I'm not here to leave behind a legacy of depletion. I'm here to win big and do good through my Soul's dream — and to show other Heart Leaders how to do the same, so they too can be part of the total circulation of love they pour into the world.

When asked, "Nadia, what do you mean by *From Dreaming to Done – A Soul Map for Finishing What You Were Born to Do*?" I respond like this:

Almost everyone I meet through my work has a secret dream: the dream of being number one in their life. But not everyone has the tools to develop true ambition or leave their comfort zone.

In my work as a guide and mentor, I teach Heart Leaders how to turn their desire to be number one into concrete results — without losing their essence and without giving up when the path is longer than expected or takes a different turn.

I help these dreamers see things through to the end. To develop the kind of perseverance that's rooted in clarity. Usually, they leave behind the run-of-the-mill conditioning of their old life plan and step into their truest selves.

My business card could say this:

Perseverance and stamina, coupled with clarity — for dreamers.

And we learn how to do all of this while having fun and living fully, filled with the pleasure of being our authentic, natural selves in full-spectrum rainbow colors.

Here Are the 9 Chimes of Your Soul Calling You to Finish What You Were Born to Do:

1. **Listen to the Calling** – The siren song in your heart pointing you to your Soul's North Star.

2. **Cultivate the Connection** – Your vision and your soul desire clarity.

3. **Build Consistency** – By honoring your voice and needs.

4. **Gain Clarity** – Listen to your HeArt.

5. **Follow Your Conviction** – Access your personal power.

6. **Practice Clearing** – Release your womb from the expectations of others.
   The womb, beyond its biological function, holds potent symbolism across cultures and spiritual traditions. It represents creation, fertility, and the divine feminine — a source of life, potential, and inner wisdom. It is also linked to

birth, transformation, and renewal, mirroring the cyclical nature of life and reconnecting us to the natural world and to ourselves.

7. **Master Your Confidence** – Learn to trust yourself, your life, and your gifts.

8. **Master Compassion** – Understand that true compassion is born from self-love leadership. When you become highly skilled in self-compassion, self-forgiveness, and self-love, even against all odds, you become proficient in Self-Love Leadership. You understand the value of gentle courage and the strength of compassion when fully embodied. Mastery implies not only knowing how to do something but doing it consistently and with integrity. This is what it means to be a Heart Leader, walking your talk and taking your own medicine, unwavering in your self-love.

9. **Celebrate** – Stop and smell the roses.

Most importantly, don't forget to celebrate your milestones — often. [This is the Done / Integration stage of the Spiral — where honoring and celebrating the journey anchors your mission in joy.] Don't downplay your accomplishments or let your inner critic say, "It's nothing." Watch out for that conditioned voice that whispers, "It's not enough" or

"It's too much to celebrate. Who are you to do that?"

Don't listen, my beautiful friend. CELEBRATE every chance you get.

Let's do a little celebration exercise right now. Don't be shy about celebrating. Don't hold back. And whatever you do, don't dim your light when it's time to toot your horn. This is just between you and you, no one else needs to know.

If this next exercise feels challenging, simply notice where you feel it in your body. Those little pings you're sensing? They're just information.

Approach this exercise with a curious heart, one that's ready to celebrate your beYOUty. Yes, Beauty.

Celebrate Your BeYOUty in Love & Appreciation

Finish these sentences from the space of love, gratitude, the heart, and valuing yourself and all you offer.

The Mirror is You: Your Spirit Action

I like myself because...
The thing I do best is...
My best quality is...
My special talent is...

I feel proud when...
The most important thing to know about me...
What makes me unique is...
The thing I like best about myself...
The universe loves me because...

If I was introduced to someone right now, the first great thing they would notice about me is...

I want to honor and acknowledge that I received this exercise from my Soul Sister, Zinnia Gupte of shaktipriestess.com, co-author of the compilation book *The Wisdom of Midlife Women 2*, in which we both shared our stories.

Testimonial/Case Study
Soul Heart Session Power Mantra

Before the session, I felt dizzy in the brain with my mind running round and round through all the things that still need fixing, doing, and resolving. I thought to myself: "At least I said "yes" to this one good thing, a spiritual and creative journey with Nadia!"

I had no idea what that would be like but I was going to let go and participate. I was excited about the potential.

During the session, it felt good to be heard. It felt safe, to be honest. It felt good to take this overview journey of my life and slowly go deeper with it. I had the sense of the possibility that I was coming to a point of clarity.

On completion, I feel calm, clear, and centered in my intention to focus on my path and allow the Spirit to bring everything through the energy of gratitude even before any evidence of manifestation.

Nadia, as my guide, led me through the maze of life to lift the fog, and I was able to access my Soul's wisdom which landed quite viscerally in my body. My Soul Power Mantra is: "I am so happy and grateful now that Spirit is the Power in my life."

Judy McNutt, the Holistic Book Coach
JudyMcNutt.com

What echoes in you from her story?

3 Key Takeaways

1. **You are the creator of your reality** – not a victim of it. By understanding and stepping out of the Drama Triangle, you can reclaim your agency and align with your Soul's mission.

2. **The Magic Three (Soul Desire, Soul Fire, Soul Medicine)** are essential for consistent, soul-aligned follow-through. They provide clarity, stamina, and emotional balance for fulfilling your dream.

3. **Following through is a sacred act of Self-Love Leadership**. It requires courage, consistency, and celebration. When you trust your inner wisdom and lead with heart, you finish what you were born to do.

Chapter Recap

- **Your dream matters** — and it requires more than just positive thinking; it demands follow-through rooted in soul-aligned action.

- **The Drama Triangle** (Victim, Persecutor, Rescuer) explains the unconscious dynamics that sabotage your mission. Awareness helps you exit these roles and reclaim your power.

- **Your turning point begins with a "No"** —

setting boundaries might trigger others, but it initiates your liberation.

- **The Magic Three**:

    ◦ **Ignite Soul Desire**: Reconnect with your dream again and again.

    ◦ **Harness Soul Fire**: Channel your energy into aligned, purposeful action.

    ◦ **Apply Soul Medicine**: Pause to breathe, rest, and listen inward.

- **Soul Desires act as your compass** when clarity fades.

- **Consistency comes from aligned action**, not hustle.

- **Self-trust, gentle courage, and personal truth** are the keys to lasting transformation.

- **You are a Herzensmensch and Lebenskünstler** — a heart-centered human and artist of life. These qualities are your strength, not liabilities.

- **The 9 Chimes of Your Soul** guide you through every phase of completing your sacred mission — from the initial calling to the celebration of your fulfilled dream.

Celebrate often and fully. It's not ego; it's energy. Celebration is how you integrate, embody, and honor your path.

As you close this chapter, notice where you've already followed through with gentle courage — and where you may be ready to step into the Expression Gate yourself. Following through isn't about force; it's about igniting your desire, harnessing your fire, applying your medicine, and celebrating the milestones along the way. You've now touched Integration — the place where your mission becomes embodied joy. In the next chapter, we'll deepen into what it means to live as Joy in Motion — the celebration of a dream fulfilled and a life fully claimed.

CHAPTER SEVEN
Dare to Dream

"When a flower doesn't bloom, you fix the environment in which it grows, not the flower."
— Alexander Den Heijer

It was my dad who dared me to dream when he handed me that very first self-help and personal development book, *You Can If You Think You Can*. He planted the seed when he asked me, "What would you like your life to be like?" [This was my Dreamspark — the seed of daring to dream planted in the Spiral.]

Although he wasn't able to provide the environment I needed to bloom, one grounded in stability, security, and safety, he did give me something meaningful: the right seeds. During those formative years between ages 11 and 13, his influence laid the foundation. From 14 and onward, I became the one to water, nurture, and fertilize those seeds so they could bloom gloriously. [This was my Soul Yes — a choice to honor the dream even without stable ground.]

Not every soil I planted them in allowed them to blossom. So I carried those seeds with me, searching for the right environment where they would.

From Dreaming to Living as Joy in Motion

Because of that seed — *You Can If You Think You Can* — I had an experience at age 14 that I now recognize as a spiritual awakening and profound awareness. This awakening would eventually lead me to speak of *The Magic of Transformation* at age 32, publish a book about it at age 46, and at age 47, give that awareness a name: *Soul Health*. That same year, I launched a podcast to spread the word. [Here, I stepped into the Spiral again, turning awakening into creation and service.]

Have you ever wondered what it feels like when self-care stops being a duty and becomes a sacred dialogue with your Soul? When self-care becomes *Soul Care*, not just another item on your to-do list, but a way of *being*?

On the *Soul Health Mentor Podcast*, I hold sacred space to help you remember how to care for your whole self, not in fragments, but in sacred wholeness. How to transform your lived experience, not by forcing change, but by harmonizing your subtle bodies.

Your life is not just physical.

It is a *symphony* of bodies, each whispering their truth:

- **Your Physical Body** — the sacred vessel of your Soul.

- **Your Emotional Body** — the tender river of your feelings.

- **Your Mental Body** — the clarity and architecture of your thoughts.

- **Your Spirit** — the breath of life beyond the visible.

- **Your Lightbody** — the radiant memory of who you truly are.

[This is the Expression Gate — not just understanding, but embodying Soul Health in full symphony.]

Cultivating Soul Health is learning how to nourish physical health and happiness, foster mental clarity and emotional balance, awaken your spiritual heart, and align with fiscal flow and soul-led prosperity. It's about *embodying* your Soul's unique health and purpose, a sacred homecoming to the full symphony of *you*.

The magic of transformation is the realization of our true self. It supports the successful expression of our fundamental personality, our desires, and our potential, aligned with our being and the laws of nature.

Like the caterpillar-to-butterfly metamorphosis, *The Magic of Transformation* follows a divine plan, honoring the sacred principles of creation. When we ignite and manifest our Soul Desires, divine intention and consciousness flow through us.

Your Soul Health in Full Expression

The fullness of your Soul Health expression might look like you, joyful and alive, jumping across a beach in a bathing suit. Intoxicated by vitality, you soar with wings and roots. A way of being where the seven keystone areas in body, mind, heart, and spirit align with a big, whole-body "YES!", and sometimes, a quiet, peaceful *no*, in honor of that yes. It's knowing exactly how you want to live and where you draw the line in the sand.

You Are the Mirror: The 7 Keystone Questions

Do you ever wonder what it would feel like to:

- Feel great most of the time, balanced and whole?

- Wake up each morning looking forward to the day?

- Love the work you do, give it your all, and still have energy for pleasure and play?

- Look terrific and feel amazing about yourself?

- And your life?

- Know you have everything you need to face whatever comes your way?

Sounds like a utopian dream?

It's not. It's within reach.

It's called *The Magic of Transformation*.

From *Dreaming to Done*, anchored in *Soul Health* expression.

You've got this.

You know why? Because *you* are the artist and creator of your life.

Your Soul Map isn't a strategy.

It's your **Original Divine Soul Blueprint**, an invitation to remember who you truly are.

This blueprint holds your unique answers to the three most essential questions:

1. Who am I?

2. Why am I here?

3. What's my purpose?

You don't have to walk this path alone.

This book can guide you. I can guide you.

It's my craft. It's what I'm here for.

Dear Heart & Soul: A Love Note to You

You, beautiful heart and brilliant Soul, are:

- **Creative**, by nature
- **Whole**, by design
- **Powerful**, by claim
- **Magic**, by heArt
- **Sexy**, by Empowered Body
- **Talented**, by applying your Soul's gifts

You are called to live your dream by *finishing*

what you started. Completing your dream *by Soul's Design* will allow you to *be* who you were born to be. And one thing I know for sure:

You were born to be creative, to restore wholeness in yourself and others, to claim your power for what truly matters, and to BE magical, sexy, talented, beYOUtiful YOU.

[This is Done/Integration — the Spiral landing in your heart, affirming that you are whole and capable of living your dream.]

Testimonial/Casestudy

Healthy Boundaries in South Africa!

From people-pleasing tendencies to creating better boundaries

"Before doing the Akashic Soul Realignment® work with Nadia, I could sense that I wasn't functioning at my best. There were behaviors and habits that were preventing me from thriving.

Beginning the Soul Realignment® work, I was a bit nervous at first but Nadia delivered the information in such a gentle way and with such care.

After completing the 3-Step Soul Realignment® Power Retrieval Process with Nadia, I notice my tendency to 'people please' a lot more easily and am able to 'step back' and evaluate before responding. I used to worry a lot more about what people thought of me, but I'm finding it easier to put boundaries in place.

I highly recommend working with Nadia in a 1:1 setting because of the way she is able to share information that takes a minute to digest. She always did so in a gentle and caring way.

Doing this Akashic Soul Realignment® work is incredibly informative and enlightening and also a truly beautiful (and beneficial) thing to feel so 'seen'. "

- Tam, South Africa

What echoes in you from her story?

3 Key Takeaways:

1. **Seeds of transformation begin with a dream**, even if the environment is imperfect,

the right mindset and internal cultivation can lead to lasting change.

2. **Soul Health is a multidimensional way of being**, true self-care involves harmonizing your physical, emotional, mental, spiritual, and energetic bodies.

3. **You are the creator of your life**, transformation happens when you remember your divine blueprint and fully express your Soul's purpose.

Chapter Recap:

- Dreaming awakens when you believe in your potential, no matter your external circumstances.

- Seeds of Soul Health grow when nurtured with care and aligned with the right environment.

- Spiritual awakenings often spark the birth of new concepts, visions, or life paths.

- Self-care becomes Soul Care when practiced across your five bodies: physical, emotional, mental, spiritual, and lightbody.

- True transformation aligns your Soul's desires with divine timing and natural laws, much like a caterpillar becoming a butterfly.

- Living Soul Health in full expression means embodying joy, balance, vitality, and conscious choice — where your "yes" and "no" are sacred.

- The 7 Keystone Questions guide you toward alignment and wholeness.

- Your Soul Map is not a strategy but a recalling, answering: Who am I? Why am I here? What is my purpose?

- Always remember: you are creative, magical, and powerful — here to complete what only you were born to express.

Spirit Action: **What is one bold and courageous step you will take in the direction of your dream come true?**

[This keeps the Spiral alive — completion is not an end, but ongoing motion into your next sacred yes.]

As you close this chapter, notice how your Dreamspark has never left you. You've said your Soul Yes, spiraled deeper into awakening, and expressed your Soul Health in tangible ways. Now, you stand in Done/Integration — remembering you are already the artist of your life. In the next chapter, we turn toward the legacy of Joy in Motion, exploring how finishing your dream allows you to live not just for yourself, but as part of a greater circulation of love.

Conclusion

"When you recover or discover something that nourishes your soul and brings you joy, care enough about yourself to make room for it in your life."
— Jean Shinoda Bolen

Your Dream is a Living Soul Map

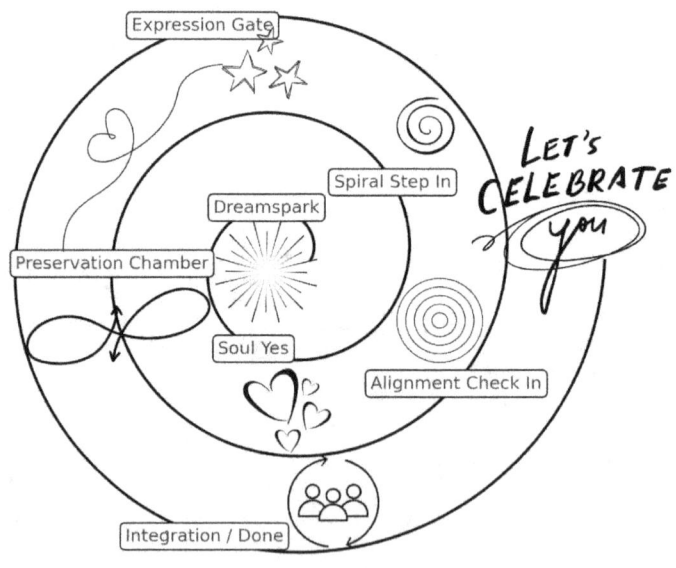

Soul Map Spiral ™ Process

Methodology by Nadia S. Krauss
Soul Health Mentor & Co

The Soul Map Spiral™ Process — 7 Layers from Dreamspark to Done/Integration

A visual guide to locate yourself, choose a loving next step, and return again as you evolve.

1. **Dreamspark** — The first flicker. A body-based nudge that says "this matters."

2. **Soul Yes** — Your conscious, embodied consent to the dream.

3. **Spiral Step In** — Begin moving; small aligned action replaces waiting.

4. **Preservation Chamber** — Protect the spark: rest, heal, simplify, resource.

5. **Alignment Checkpoint** — Discernment: release what's not you, reaffirm what is.

6. **Expression Gate** — Share the dream in form (words, offers, art, service).

7. **Done / Integration** — Harvest, celebrate, integrate—and listen for the next spark.

How to use this map (right now):

1. **Locate yourself:** Place a finger on the layer that feels most true today.

2. **Name the need:** Ask, "What would love do

here?" Write one sentence.

3. **Take one step:** Choose a micro-action you can complete in 24–72 hours. Celebrate.

You've journeyed through this book and through it you connected to your Soul Map Spiral™ of remembering, one that doesn't move in straight lines or predictable steps, but rather in sacred rhythms and soul truths.

Along the way, you've discovered that:

- Your dream is not something outside of you, but within you — evolving, shapeshifting, deepening as you do.

- Expression is healing. The act of creating, coloring, reflecting, and speaking your truth is how your dream breathes and grows.

- Milestones aren't achievements; they're soul markers, sacred signposts of your growth, clarity, and courage.

- Emotional resilience is the soil, not the absence of pain, but your rooted capacity to return to your truth, again and again, with grace.

- Spirit Action is the water that nurtures the development of your dream. Simple, intentional steps that nourish your vision and bring your inner world into outer expression.

- Embodiment is your crown. The lived devotion of walking with your dream, rooted in your body, led by your soul, and in loving conversation with your heart.

This book is not the end of your journey. It's a mirror, a map, a mandala. Reminding you that your Heroine's Path is not about striving or proving, but becoming. Becoming the one who lives her dream now, not perfectly, but presently. Becoming the change you wish to see in the world. You already hold the medicine you seek. You already are the Soul Artist of your life.

So walk forward.

One spiral at a time.

One sacred step.

One embodied truth.

Your dream has been waiting for you to walk with it while you remember to finish what you were born to be.

Author's Note
A Love Letter to You, Dreamwalker

"I must be a mermaid. I have no fear of depth and a great fear of shallow living." — Anais Nin

---

Dear Soul Sister (or Brother) on the Path,

Thank you.

From the bottom of my heart, thank you for walking this journey with me - not just reading the words, but letting them speak to your bones, stir your truth, and awaken what your heart and soul still hold dear.

You didn't just read a book.

You walked a spiral of remembering.

You heard the call. You dared to begin. You said yes.

Each chapter has been a sacred step of becoming

and of un-becoming who you were told to be, and recalling who you truly are:

You heard the call, that quiet longing from within that whispered, *"There is more."*

You initiated the shift, stepping out of your comfort zone and into your sacred discomfort.

You cultivated the practice, learning to honor the divine timing, not force the bloom.

You did the work, clearing patterns, rewriting stories, reclaiming your truth.

You walked the talk, giving yourself permission to live your dream, out loud.

You embraced gentle courage, not the roar, but the rooted whisper that says, *I'm ready.*

You moved from dreaming to living, not as a destination, but as Joy in Motion.

If there's one message I want to leave you with, it's this:

You are the dream you came here to fulfill.

You are the one you've been looking for.

You are the medicine you've been waiting for.

Your life is art. Your path is sacred.

Do not die with a dream still living inside you.

This is not goodbye — it's a threshold.

If this book spoke to your Soul, I warmly invite you to go deeper.

You are welcome to join me for:

A Soul Map Journey – A 10 Minute Ritual for Returning to Your Dreams

→ https://bit.ly/SoulMapGift

The Soul's Calling – a 3-day immersive retreat to deepen your clarity — activate your intuitive gifts, and align with your dream "done." From root to rise.

→ https://bit.ly/FromDreamingToDoneRetreat

The Soul's Pathway – a 9-month guided spiral of support where we walk together, month by month, integrating your vision into embodied reality, with ritual, reflection, nourishment and aligned spirit action.

→ https://bit.ly/9-MonthMentorship

Your next sacred step is waiting.

I'd be honored to walk beside you.

With infinite gratitude, gentle courage, and a full heart,

Nadia S. Krauss

Artist. Guide. Dream Finisher

Soul Health Mentor & Co. Business. As Sacred. As Service. As Revolution.

Thank You for Reading

Dear Heart Leader,

Thank you for taking the time to journey through the pages of this book. It means the world to me that you chose to spend your precious energy walking with the stories, reflections, and soul work I've poured into these chapters.

If this book has touched your heart, sparked a new awareness, or supported you in any part of your Soul's journey, I'd be deeply grateful if you'd consider leaving an honest review.

Your voice matters, not just to me, but to other readers who may be searching for the very medicine this book offers.

- Your review helps others discover this work

- It helps me continue sharing stories that heal, empower, and inspire

- And it keeps the spiral dance of connection going, reader to reader, heart to heart, soul to soul

Thank you again for being here. For showing up. For remembering.

With love and gratitude,
Nadia S. Krauss
Soul Artist. Guide. Author. Speaker. Podcast Host.

https://www.happywholesomelife.com/

https://soulhealthmentor.com/

About the Author

Nadia S. Krauss is a Soul Health Mentor, author, speaker, and Dream Finisher. She helps heart-led women leaders go from "I hope it happens someday" to "It is done — in truth, in power, in presence."

As founder of Soul Health Mentor & Co., she weaves sacred structure with soul expression, guiding her clients to complete the dreams that have lived inside them for too long. Her work stands at the intersection of creative expression, devotional discipline, holistic embodiment, and regenerative leadership.

Her mission: to root women into the safety of their knowing — and rise with them into the richest version of their lives.

Through her writing, *Soul Art® creations, retreats, and mentorship, Nadia holds space for what she calls the sacred completion cycle — when a long-held vision finally takes form.

*Soul Art® is a registered trademark owned by Soul Art Studio and refers specifically to the Soul Art® processes taught in the Soul Art Certification.

Email: nadia@happywholesomelife.com

FB: https://www.facebook.com/nadiaskrauss/

Acknowledgements

When the personality comes fully to serve the energy of its soul that is authentic empowerment."
– Gary Zukov

Surround yourself with joyful people who believe in magic, and magically heartfelt people who believe in the kind of happiness that comes from fully serving the energy of your heart and soul. Do this through your personality, divine gifts, and talents, which are already leading the way for you to embody your true nature.

At the very center of this truth is the love of my life, Eric, who for the last 30 years has never stopped believing in me, investing in me, and reminding me of the power of our love, no matter how imperfect. His steadfast love and support is the bedrock upon which all of this is built.

I feel so blessed to be working and co-creating with so many Heart Leaders in the beautiful city of Ottawa. I want to begin by honoring two such Heart Leaders: Samantha Moonsammy Gordon and Simar

El Nounou from Lucky Book Publishing.

Thank you to all the incredible LBP authors in my community. I'm deeply grateful to interview you on my Soul Health Mentor Podcast, alongside other changemakers and Heart Leaders.

I still remember Samantha Moonsammy-Gordon delivering an inspiring keynote at an event called *Dream Big. Change the World*, a gathering for both local and global leaders, created by the amazing Lisa Anna Palmer of LightYourLeadership.com. Samantha invited us to imagine what the world could look like if good women had the money — good people with wealth, winning big and doing good in the world. It lit a fire in all of us.

And now, I'm witnessing the powerful ripple effect that we, as women, can create. Wow.

I feel deep gratitude for all the new connections this chapter of my life, in Ottawa, Ontario, Canada, is making possible, and for the vibrant Lucky Book Publishing community I now call home. I'm honored to be building such rich relationships, anchored in a rich life, in more ways than one.

What a gift it is to be part of this cosmic alignment, where changemakers rise together to impact the world with positive change while rooting for one another.

Land Acknowledgment Across My Soul's Journey

This book is born of many lands. Each one has shaped my soul, sculpted my story, and contributed to the dream I now dare to live. With reverence, I honor the ancestral stewards of the lands that held me, raised me, and called me home.

To the Algonquin Anishinaabe Nation, caretakers of the unceded territory of Ottawa, Canada, where I now live and create — thank you. Your deep connection to the land, waters, and Spirit infuses my path with purpose and remembrance. I offer my deepest respect and gratitude for your wisdom, resilience, and continued presence.

To Muscogee (Creek) peoples, original stewards of what is now known as Albany, Georgia, where I lived for over eight years, I offer thanks. Honoring the ancestral wisdom of highly skilled agricultural trade and mound-building. As well as upholding the importance of ongoing communication with ancestors and deceased loved ones, to receive guidance.

To the Khoe and San peoples of Cape Town, South Africa, where my mother grew up and where I lived for a few seasons, I honor your ancient knowledge, sacred language, and enduring spirit. The mountains, ocean, and wind there taught me about deep time and ancestral memory.

To the Indigenous peoples of what is now called Stuttgart, Germany, where I was born, including the Celts and various tribal peoples of Swabia, I acknowledge the ancient rhythms that pulse beneath the modern cityscape. Though often forgotten or obscured, these roots continue to whisper of old ways, deep knowing, and Spirit-led belonging.

Across each of these lands, I acknowledge the beauty and the pain, the brokenness and the brilliance, the colonization and the continuation of life. I walk forward with humility and gratitude, committed to honoring the Earth, uplifting Indigenous voices, and co-creating a world that remembers its sacred origins.

May this work be an offering toward collective healing, truth, and transformation.

Blessing for the Dreamer Who Finishes

Prayer for the Closing Chapter
May the lands that shaped you rise to bless your becoming.
May your dream be finished in truth,
and your heart always return to its sacred home.

thank you

Dear Reader,

You made it! Thanks for sticking with me through these pages. I hope they brought you insights and sparks of inspiration. Sharing these stories and lessons has been an incredible journey, and it means a lot that you chose to be a part of it.

Now, if I could ask a quick favour: if you enjoyed the book, would you mind leaving a positive review on Amazon or Goodreads? It would truly make my day, and it's one of the best ways to help others find this book and maybe spark their own adventures. Your review might just be the encouragement someone else needs to give them permission to break from routine and empower them to make the change they need.

Best,

Nadia

MY GIFT TO YOU

I am so glad you're here!

As a special gift,

enjoy **FREE access** to your Soul Map Gift:
A 10-minute ritual for returning to your dreams.

https://bit.ly/SoulMapGift

www.ingramcontent.com/pod-product-compliance
Lightning Source LLC
Chambersburg PA
CBHW061800120626

46550CB00005B/2078